# GENETIC IMAGINATIONS: ETHICAL, LEGAL AND SOCIAL ISSUES IN HUMAN GENOME RESEARCH

# Genetic Imaginations: Ethical, Legal and Social Issues in Human Genome Research

*Edited by*
PETER GLASNER and HARRY ROTHMAN
*Centre for Social and Economic Research*
*University of the West of England, Bristol*

# Ashgate

Aldershot • Brookfield USA • Singapore • Sydney

Published by
Ashgate Publishing Limited,
Gower House,
Croft Road,
Aldershot,
Hants GU11 3HR,
England

Ashgate Publishing Company,
Old Post Road,
Brookfield,
Vermont 05036,
USA

Ashgate website:http://www.ashgate.com

Reprinted 1999

**British Library Cataloguing in Publication Data**
Genetic imaginations: ethical, legal and social issues in
    human genome research
    1. Human genetics - Research  2. Human genetics - Moral and
    ethical aspects
    I. Glasner, Peter E. (Peter Egan)  II. Rothman, Harry
    176.2'5

**Library of Congress Catalog Card Number:** 98-070154

ISBN 1 84014 356 8

Printed in Great Britain by Biddles Limited
Guildford and King's Lynn

# Contents

# Acknowledgements

We would like to thank the Centre for Social and Economic Research at the University of the West of England for hosting the Workshop on which this book is based, and Carfax Publishing Ltd for their contribution to the costs. We would also like to thank Carfax and the editor for allowing us to reprint the contents of a double issue of *The Genetic Engineer and Biotechnologist* 15 2/3: 83-187, 1995, in which these papers first appeared, for dissemination to a wider audience, and Christine Taylor for sorting out the typing so efficiently.

Peter Glasner and Harry Rothman,
Bristol, 1997.

# List of Contributors

Brian Balmer

Lecturer, Department of History, Philosophy and Communication of Science, University College, London WC1E 6BT

Jean-Paul Gaudillière

Research Fellow, Institut National de la Santé et de la Recherche Médicale, 75743, Paris, Cedex 15, France.

Peter Glasner

Research Professor in Sociology, Centre for Social and Economic Research, University of the West of England, Bristol BS16 1QY.

Christine Hine

Research Fellow, Centre for Research into Innovation Culture and Technology, Brunel University, Uxbridge, Middlesex UB8 3PH.

Paul Martin

Research Fellow, Science Policy Research Unit, University of Sussex, Falmer, Brighton, Sussex BN1 9RF.

Ruth McNally

Research Fellow, Centre for Research into Innovation Culture and Technology, Brunel University, Uxbridge, Middlesex UB8 3PH.

Hilary Rose

Professor Emerita of Social Policy, University of Bradford, Bradford BD7 1DP.

Harry Rothman

Professor of Science and Technology Policy, School of Sociology, University of the West of England, Bristol BS16 1QY.

David Travis

Senior Lecturer in Sociology, University of Glamorgan, Pontypridd, South Wales CF37 1DL.

Jon Turney

Senior Lecturer, Department of History, Philosophy and Communication of Science, University College, London WC1E 6BT

Peter R. Wheale

Lecturer, Surrey European Management School, University of Surrey, Guildford, Surrey GU2 5XH.

# 1 Social Dimensions of the Human Genome Mapping Project: An Introduction

PETER GLASNER & HARRY ROTHMAN

## Background

There is now a considerable secondary literature on the attempt to identify, characterise and ultimately sequence all of the estimated 100 000 genes in the human genome (see *inter alia* Bishop and Waldholz (1990), Cook-Degan (1994), Davis (1991), Kevles and Hood (1992), Wingerson (1990) and articles in this book). This formidable task has transformed molecular biology into 'big science' (de Solla Price 1963) and will take at least another 10 years to complete. According to the Office of Science and Technology (OST, 1994, p.6), the Human Genome Mapping Programme "has enormous potential for the improvement of health and wealth creation". It has become a focus for study by social as well as natural scientists because, unlike many of the other new technologies, genetics most directly affects all of us at a very personal level. Mills (1970, p.12) saw the essential project of social science as the use of the imagination to "grasp history and biography and the relations between the two in society". This enables the social scientist "to range from the most impersonal and remote transformations to the most intimate features of the human self". Hence, his concern for the relationship between "the personal troubles of milieu" and "the public issues of social structure" strikes a resonant chord in the project to find what has been described as the 'holy grail' of genetics.

The sequencing of all of the 3000 million base pairs which constitute the human genome requires a major international effort, with key players located primarily in the US, Europe and Japan. British participation has been justified primarily on two grounds (OST, 1994, p.11); the existence of a strong tradition of important work in the field of genetics which has allowed significant and rapid progress to be made within relatively constrained resources; and the ability of the

1

UK expertise to exploit the health-related findings to improve diagnostic techniques, and thereby relieve some of the financial burdens on the National Health Service (NHS). The social, legal and ethical issues, however, have been left to other organisations to consider, including the Human Genome Organisation (HUGO), which has them as parts of its brief (Glasner, 1993), and the Nuffield Council on Bioethics, which published a report on the ethical issues in genetic screening in 1993 (Nuffield Council on Bioethics, 1993). However, the recent government White Paper, 'Realising our Potential' (HMSO, 1993), refers not only to the importance of innovation and wealth creation, but also of the quality of life, and the need to improve the public understanding of science.

## The Scientific Issues

The key scientific issues for the continuing development of the Human Genome Mapping Project (HGMP) in Britain are summarised in the OST report (1994) as:

- Genetic mapping - the need to complete a genetic map at a level of resolution to permit identification of the genes involved in disease, and to collect family material through the NHS.
- Physical mapping - continuing to expand the development of Yeast Artificial Chromosome (YAC)-based physical maps, and soliciting proposals for the use of other vectors to improve resolution.
- Comparative mapping - enlarging the scope to include maps of agriculturally important species as the basis for crop and livestock improvement.
- DNA sequencing - funding the sequencing of gene-rich regions of the human genome with all sequence data placed in the public domain.
- Genome informatics - improving the efficiency, management and accessibility of database communication and software development.
- Commercial opportunities - the facilitation of technology transfer to the biotechnology, pharmaceutical and agricultural industries in order to benefit the nation as a whole.
- Public education and training - the necessity for an appropriate infrastructure to be developed to allow the greatest exploitation of data for the benefit of the health of the nation.

## The Social Issues

The issues for social scientists appear rather different. There is much debate about the reductionist nature of a programme which relates many social characteristics to elements in human genetic make-up (Lewontin, 1993; Rose, 1994, Chapter 8; Rothman, 1995). The impact on new reproductive technologies has become the focus of concern for a variety of feminist social science analyses (Stanworth, 1987; Spallone & Steinberg, 1987; McNeill *et al.*, 1990; Stacey, 1992). The possibility of employment-based discrimination based on genetic analysis has also raised doubts and not only among social scientists, especially with the advent of AIDS (Nelkin & Tancredi, 1989). The use of DNA fingerprinting in areas of social life ranging from paternity suits to crime detection appears to have transformed some aspects of policing and the law (Lander, 1992). In addition, the possibility that commercial organisations may wish to patent the results of the Human Genome Project - patenting 'life' itself - has led to debate at the highest scientific as well as social levels (Anderson, 1992; Cornwell, 1992; Roberts, 1992). Finally, there is now a rapidly growing field of genetic ethics or 'genethics' (Suzuki & Knudtson, 1990) dealing with the more fundamental issues raised by the HGMP while recognising that few, if any, are peculiar to this branch of molecular biology.

Other issues are addressed in the following papers, based on a workshop held in the Centre for Social and Economic Research at the University of the West of England, Bristol in February 1995. It was organised by the authors of this paper, and followed similar workshops held in Holland the previous year and at the British Sociological Association's Annual Conference the year before. Participants from the fields of the social studies of science and technology, and science policy studies, were invited from the UK and France to give work-in-progress presentations and provide constructive and critical feedback on the social, political and ethical issues in human genome research. A number of revised papers have been included here covering most of the topics discussed.

The approaches of the authors derive in the main from recent advances in the field of science and technology studies (Glasner & Rothman, 1994; Jasanoff *et al.*, 1994). A variety of research methods, including interviews, surveys, ethnographies and documentary analysis, have been used, often with several methods in each study as a way of improving the validity and reliability of the results through triangulation (Denzin, 1970).

The papers that follow go some way to deconstructing the unspoken rationality noted by Webster (1991, p.41) in his discussion of the relationship between the social studies of science and government science policies, and showing its limitations in the context of the HGMP.   He concludes that such policies are based on the assumptions:

> ... that scientific knowledge can be treated as a 'black box' and managed on behalf of society; that expert authorities can advise on this process; that indicators of how successful this process is are available; and finally, that adequate regulatory safe-guards can be built into the process.

The four papers by Balmer, Gaudillière, Hine and Glasner *et al.* are primarily concerned to understand the processes which take place within the 'black box' of science and technology.  Balmer argues that traditional research sites and practices are being supplemented by newer and more varied forms of knowledge production, and uses the Resource Centre of the UK HGMP as an example of this process. Glasner *et al.* also focus on this Centre to draw lessons for future policy in relation to differing modes of management and organisation of genetic research.  Hine, an ethnographer, reports a study of the use of information technology of IT as a scientific instrument providing a new window on nature.  Gaudillière suggests that scientific advances in genetics are beginning to have profound effects on clinical practice, and reports on a study of these changes within a Paris clinic.

The papers by McNally and Wheale look at the implications of the HGMP through the expertise of lawyers and medical geneticists.  McNally suggests that decisions by pregnant women concerning their unborn fetuses will increasingly need to be taken in the light of recent advances in medical genetics. Wheale uses Rawls' concept of reflective equilibrium as a heuristic tool with which to explore the ethics now embodied in the medico-legal framework for conception, embryo research, fetal tissue transplantation and pregnancy termination. Indicators of the success of the programme for society as a whole through commercial exploitation are explored by Martin, who examines the development of gene therapy in the US by focusing on the key role dedicated gene therapy firms are playing in creating this radical new technology.

Finally, the problems of establishing regulatory safeguards as exemplified by a better-informed public are explored by Rose and Turney.  Rose suggests that the notion of a socially shaped science and technology has placed the consideration of wider public participation in its future development on the social agenda. Turney argues that prevailing models of scientific literacy are flawed because they assume that it is only scientists who can define what people should know about science.  He seeks to develop a more useful concept of genetic literacy in contests where people who might need access to genetic information play a more significant part in the process.  These papers are examples of current social science research which address the issues raised by the HGMP and attempt, contrary to the fears of some practitioners (for example, Vickers 1994), to provide some answers so that progress may continue in an environment of informed debate within society as a whole.

## References

Anderson, C. (1992) US genome head faces charges of conflict. *Nature*, **356,** 453.

Bishop, J.E. & Waldholz, M. (1990) *Genome-The Story of the Most Astonishing Adventure of our Time-The Attempt to Map All the Genes in the Human Body.* Simon and Shuster, New York.

Cook-Degan, R. (1994) *The Gene Wars: Science, Politics and the Human Genome.* Norton, London.

Cornwell, J. (1992) Gene spleen. *The Sunday Times Magazine,* 26 July.

Davis, J. (1991) *Mapping the Code: The Human Genome Project and the Choices of Modern Science.* Wiley, New York.

Denzin, N. (1970) *The Research Act in Sociology.* Butterworths, London.

de Solla Price, D. (1963) *Little Science, Big Science.* Columbia University Press, New York.

Glasner, P.E. (1993) Programming nature and public participation in decision making: a European perspective. In Durant, J. & Gregory, J. (eds) *Science and Culture in Europe.* The Science Museum, London.

Glasner, P.E. & Rothman, H. (1994) Science studies: a guide for strategic management. *Technology Analysis and Strategic Management,* **6,** 505-525.

HMSO (1993) Realising our Potential - A Strategy for Science and Technology, Cmnd 2250. HMSO, London.

Jasanoff, S., Markle, G.E., Petersen, J.C. & Pinch, T. (1994) *Handbook of Science and Technology Studies.* Sage, London.

Kevles, D.J. & Hood, L. (1992) *The Code of Codes: Scientific and Social Issues in the Human Genome Project.* Harvard University Press, Cambridge, MA.

Lander, E. (1992) DNA fingerprinting. Science, law and the ultimate identifier. In Kevles & Hood (1992), 191-210.

Lewontin, R.C. (1993) *The Doctrine of DNA. Biology as Ideology.* Penguin, Harmondsworth.

McNeill, M., Varcoe, I. & Yearley, S. (1990) *The New Reproductive Technologies.* Macmillan, London.

Mills, C.W. (1970) *The Sociological Imagination.* Penguin. Harmondsworth.

Nelkin, D. & Tancredi, L. (1989) *Dangerous Diagnostics: The Social Power of Biological Information.* Basic Books, New York.

Nuffield Council on Bioethics (1993) *Genetic Screening-Ethical Issues.* The Nuffield Foundation, London.

OST (1994) *The Human Genome Mapping Project in the UK. Priorities and Opportunities in Genome Research.* Office of Science and Technology, HSMO, London.

Roberts, L. (1992) Why Watson quit as project head. *Science,* **256,** 310-312.

Rose, H. (1994) *Love, Power and Knowledge. Towards a Feminist Transformation of the Sciences.* Routledge, London.

Rothman, B.K. (1995) Of maps and imaginations: sociology confronts the genome. *Social Problems,* **42,** 1-10.

Spallone, P. & Steinberg, D.L. (1987) *Made to Order. The Myth of Reproductive and Genetic Progress.* Pergamon, Oxford.

Stacey, M. (1992) *Changing Human Reproduction: Social Perspectives.* Sage, London.

Stanworth, M. (1987) *Reproductive Technologies: Gender, Motherhood and Medicine.* Polity, Cambridge.

Suzuki, D & Knudtson, P. (1990) *Genethics: The Ethics of Engineering Life.* Harvard University Press, Cambridge, MA.

Vickers, T. (1994) The Human Genome Project. *The Genetic Engineer and Biotechnologist,* **14,** 185-194.

Webster, A. (1991) *Science, Technology and Society: New Directions.* Macmillan, London.

Wingerson, L. (1990) *Mapping our Genes: The Genome Project and the Future of Medicine.* Dutton, New York.

# 2 Transitional Science and the Human Genome Mapping Project Resource Centre

BRIAN BALMER

ABSTRACT   *Recent analysts have claimed that the science system in developed countries is in transition to a post-modern or distributed phase of organisation. Traditional research sites and practices are being supplemented by new and more varied forms of knowledge production. This chapter provides an empirical example of these changes in relation to the UK Human Genome Mapping Project. It is argued that the project Resource Centre occupies a novel position in the science system as neither a laboratory nor a warehouse for reagents. At this Centre the demands of providing a unique service have been uncoupled from the demands of a traditional research programme. One result of this process is that some employees have developed different skills and ways of innovating than they might otherwise have done in a research-based laboratory.*

## Introduction

The notion of the 'steady state' in the UK and international research system has become common parlance in the language of 1990s science policy analysis (Ziman, 1987). It is evident that the growth of the science system that occurred after the end of World War II has long since finished and that the 'research system in transition' is now the most apt description of late twentieth century science. Recent analyses have suggested that this transition might be characterised as science entering a 'post-modern' or 'distributed' stage (Crook *et al.*, 1992; Gibbons *et al.*, 1994).

Proponents of this view, such as Crook *et al*, argue that post-modernising pressures in the science system have arisen through the contraction of growth, various challenges to a single over-arching grand design for the control of nature, and an increasing emphasis on instrumental criteria for research funding decisions. Gibbons *et al.* highlight, in addition, the parallel expansion of knowledge users and knowledge producers in society as a source of change. One significant outcome of the transition, both groups of authors argue, is that traditional sites and modes of knowledge production (i.e. academic, university-based, laboratory work) start to become enmeshed in a broader, more variegated, network of institutions and practices devoted to the manufacture of knowledge. In short, a key feature of distributed, post-modern science should be the emergence of novel ways of carrying out scientific work.

Although many analysts might intuitively agree with these broad tenets of the post-modernisation theses, the arguments in its favour remain fairly abstract. This article depicts the transitional process in more concrete terms by reference to an empirical study of the Resource Centre of the UK Human Genome Mapping Project (HGMP). The HGMP, organised by the UK Medical Research Council (MRC), formed a major part of the British contribution to the international plan to map and order the entire complement of human genetic material (the genome). In terms of its organisations, the global initiative has frequently been hailed as big science for biology (Baltimore 1987; Davis, 1990), and, beyond the rhetoric, has certainly been accompanied by the hallmarks of traditional big science, including shifts towards large collaborative team efforts and expensive instrumentation. A closer examination of the UK project, based on documentary evidence and interviews with 30 scientists and policy-makers involved in the HGMP, reveals that beyond big science other changes in the organisation of genetics and molecular biology have occurred. In agreement with the post-modernisation and distributed knowledge theses, the genome project has facilitated new types of knowledge production and even created novel categories of worker.

## Gene Mapping as an Administrative Entity

The British project was initiated early in 1989 with an award of £11 million over 3 years to the MRC (Alwen, 1990; Balmer, 1993). There are a number of features of the UK situation which make the British project stand out as an unusual item of science policy. Firstly, the award was additional to the MRC grant-in-aid and was made at a time of financial stringency within civil science (Braun, 1993). A further point was that the MRC had recently been opposed to steering research, yet this initiative-along with the Council's AIDS research programme-broke with tradition and was established as a directed (i.e. mission-oriented) programme

(Smith, 1988a,b). Thirdly, the development of the UK initiative was accompanied by relatively little of the furore surrounding the launch of the US project (Wilkie, 1993, pp. 87-90).

The terms of reference for the HGMP were to "facilitate the coordination of existing activity; to expand activity in key areas; to ensure the UK is able to play a major role in the international coordination of such activity; and to ensure that the UK benefits optimally from the application and commercial exploitation of results" (MRC, 1992 p. 3). Because it had been acknowledged that the overall goal was beyond the capabilities of any one country, the British effort was to be a contribution to the global task of obtaining a complete map and sequence of the human genome (Galloway, 1990). The aims of the UK project were to be achieved mainly through two activities: a directed research programme and a separate Resource Centre.

The Directed Programme Committee (DPC) was to act as the grant-awarding committee of the project. A Project Management Committee (PMC) and Resource Centre Steering Group would oversee the operation of the Resource Centre. In addition, the PMC would have overall responsibility for the project, while ultimate responsibility lay with the MRC Cell Board and MRC Council (see Figure 1).

Communication channels between the management and project participants were also incorporated into the project structure. These chiefly took the form of annual users meetings and a quarterly newsletter entitled *G-Nome News* (called *G-String* for the first three issues).

## The Service Function of the Resource Centre

Initially located at the Clinical Research Centre in Harrow, the HGMP Resource Centre acted as a focal point for the British project. The concept had been a part of the initial project proposal and therefore was on the agenda of the project from its official commencement in April 1989. An MRC paper from a month later stated an indicative set of objectives and goals for the Centre, for example to establish ordered libraries of DNA clones, to obtain a database of genes and their map locations, and, significantly, to develop a service function to give researchers outside and others access to the information, materials and to any new methods (MRC, 1992). Despite its early prominence in the project plans, little was done to set up the Centre until after the appointment of a project manager in January 1990. After the appointment was made the following 6 months saw a business plan produced and laboratory space furnished. In June 1990 the first staff were appointed.  The Centre was budgeted to use approximately 25% of the overall HGMP budget, but European Community contracts reduced this to around 20% by June 1991 (MRC, 1991).

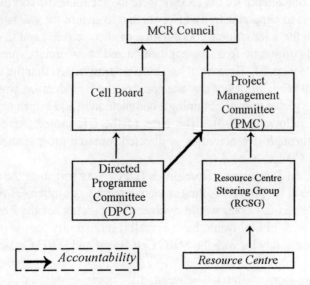

The Resource Centre undertook much of the systematic work necessary to generate materials, such as DNA probes and clones, on a scale sufficient to meet the needs of external researchers who were involved in mapping and sequencing work.  The Centre also ran the computing services which increasingly became necessary to store and process the vast amounts of data created by the initiative.  In return, registered users, who usually accessed these services free of charge, were expected-obliged in the case of project grant holders-to contribute their own results and resources to the Centre.

By undertaking this work the Resource Centre played a coordinating role within the HGMP.  First, as a source of reagents and repository of information the Centre acted as a locus for the mission of the project.  This was not just in its service capacity but additionally in what Fujimura has termed the 'standardising' of work across laboratories-sending out and receiving materials and data in a format which reduced costs and was easily transportable between locations (Fujimura, 1988).  Costs were not just economic ones in this respect.  By acting as a neutral repository, it was felt by the management that scientists would be encouraged to utilise the Centre without fear of having their data or materials misappropriated.  There was a further coordinating function of the Resource

Centre achieved through the necessity for researchers to register with the Centre in order to use it. This requirement defined and created a community of users, rather than the alternative scenario of numerous scientists engaged in *ad hoc* interactions with the Centre. Moreover, it widened the scope of the HGMP beyond the DPC grant holders to the work of a far broader community interested in aspects of gene mapping.

The geographically 'semi-centralised' project meant that the role of the Centre lay somewhere between that of a warehouse and laboratory, as a broker and facilitator of other people's work. In other words, it was not merely a repository of reagents but neither did it undertake a full research programme of its own. Moreover, the staff employed within the Centre had some previous scientific training but were not generally from academic research backgrounds (e.g from service microbiology and haematology laboratories, graduates requiring further training, from the biotechnology industry). This situation arose largely through a lack of applicants from molecular biology research rather than as a deliberate recruitment policy.

Gene mapping and sequencing involves a great amount of routine work in order to generate data. Because of this feature, the Resource Centre and the laboratories it serviced might have reflected the wider division of labour between scientists and technicians (Shapin, 1989), with the more routine and boring aspects of the work undertaken at the Centre. In the words of one DPC member and grant holder:

> ... as it's a resource centre it can employ people to do handle-cranking type jobs. I mean these are the things a research unit would have difficulty getting a grant for ... that releases labs like ours to use our resources to do the interesting things like getting really close to the gene, cloning it and doing all those things.

However, the novelty of the Resource Centre concept resulted in an equally novel division of labour, such that the Centre-laboratory relationship was not an exact reflection of the division of labour in typical laboratories. Two aspects of this phenomenon emerged in the course of interviews. The first concerned the focus of the work and the other accreditation for the work of the Centre.

### Innovation and the Resource Centre

The Resource Centre deliberately focused its work on providing a service to the scientific community. This service function was thought by the Centre management to be in conflict with pursuing an active research programme, although this line of reasoning was not the only one considered by HGMP management. It had also been suggested in earlier discussions that the Resource Centre be set up alongside an active scientific programme in order to benefit from the expertise of that programme. Another alternative had been to have wholly dispersed resources with different services attached to different laboratories. Nevertheless, the Resource Centre management decided to adopt a policy not to undertake its own research. The reason for this one member of the PMC explained, was that with any research grant there was a 'premium' for accidental discoveries, whereas with a service 'anything accidental is distracting'. Another member of the same committee made the same point more bluntly stating that: "I don't believe an average university department would have the incentives to do that (set up a production line), the first time they get to an interesting cDNA they'd have gone off and studied it".

The separation of the Resource Centre from other laboratories was an important factor in creating its unique role within the science system. From the perspective of the geneticists, the Resource Centre was there to take on the pre-biological work, what one grant holder referred to as a 'bridge to the biology', and the presence of biologists might only have resulted in the subversion of this role. In other words, spatial separation (Centre and laboratories) also entailed a social separation of roles (technicians and scientists). This, however, was a fairly idiomatic way of describing the situation. An alternative interpretation was that the need to provide a service challenged the staff to innovate in a number of ways.

In one particular respect, the experience of the Resource Centre staff with regard to their work was similar to that of research scientists. Experiments are messy, nature is recalcitrant and papers and protocols are no substitute for tacit skills for both types of work (Knorr-Cetina, 1981; Latour & Woolgar, 1979; Collins, 1985). Simply getting things to work within the context of the service function of the Resource Centre presented a challenge to the skills of its staff. The Project Manager, for example, reported that while the Resource Centre was being kitted out, "in the case of new equipment, sadly it has been the exception rather than the rule for anything to work faultlessly on the word go" (Vickers, 1990). The statement largely referred to frustration with the equipment industry. The Project Manager also described this experience with respect to the scientific techniques employed at the Centre during an interview, which it is worth quoting at length:

> ... in fact we found that if you take a standard technique, like extracting cDNA libraries, or something like that, you know the protocols are there in the literature

and everyone is quite happy with them. *But they simply don't work in the way that a production line implies. And what we've increasingly had to do ... is take these technologies and just pull them to pieces and reassemble them so that we've found out why they only work one time in five or whatever.* Now if you are in a molecular biology laboratory it doesn't matter if you just want one thing to work once, you try it several times, it works and you move on and you've got what you want out of that technology.

In more succinct terms, what it takes to count as working adequately is related to the context in which the work takes place. Moreover, quality control for users was a crucial factor in structuring the work at the Centre. Rather bluntly, if the Centre provided something which did not work they would have to deal with an angry scientist on the end of the telephone. Because of this situation, the Resource Centre can be envisaged as having taken part, not simply in the diffusion of standardised techniques and technologies, but in what Jordan and Lynch have termed their 'mainstreaming' (Jordan & Lynch, 1993). In other words, their adaptation and modification to local requirements.

Speaking with other Resource Centre staff confirmed that such mainstreaming necessitated a degree of job flexibility and innovative skills beyond that required of typical laboratory technicians. One spoke of having to 'bully robots into performing PCR' (the polymerise chain reaction used to amplify small amounts of DNA). Moreover, their comparison with other technicians was not simply with some abstract other technicians, but with colleagues working within the Clinical Research Centre associated with the Resource Centre. This point of view was echoed by the Project Manager who reported that: "experience suggests the standard of routine technical skills in a typical molecular biology laboratory is unacceptably low for the requirements of the Centre" (MRC, 1992, p.32). It is a moot point as to whether the presence and demands of an active research programme would have inhibited the innovative flexibility of the scientific support staff at the Resource Centre. The evidence presented here suggests that it might have done so. Regardless of whether or not this would have been the case, the novel context of the Resource Centre created a novel category of worker. The work required more skills (of a certain type) than those of a normal technician but less (of a certain type) than a professional scientist.

The Centre, in order to fulfil its service function, also had to undertake a limited amount of research (or less charitably, developmental work). This activity was given added impetus when the MRC Molecular Genetics Unit at Cambridge closed. This unit had been acting as an outstation of the Resource Centre with a remit to develop a new technology for the Centre. In one case the additional research performed at the Centre resulted in a patent application for a method of sorting fragments of DNA (MRC, 1992, p. 50).

The Resource Centre management appeared, somewhat inadvertently, to have created a pattern of work organisation which Senker, in a review of the literature on automation, refers to as that of the 'factory of the future' (Senker, 1992). Automation was, to some extent, a major goal of the Resource Centre. Senker argues that in order to produce maximum efficiency in automating work it is necessary to upgrade works's skills. Styles of management which concentrate on rigid working practices and assume that workers cannot possibly have the requisite skills to work with new technology lead to inefficiency (Senker, 1992; Senker & Beesley, 1986). in addition, the staff at the Centre were provided with the flexibility to deal with customers directly and without chains of bureaucratic referral. The extent to which this 'best practice' way of organising work will extend beyond the setting-up stages of the Resource Centre, and the extent to which it will survive changes in management personnel, remains to be seen.

## Reward and the Resource Centre

The novel role of the Centre also created ambiguity with regard to accreditation. Namely, if you were neither a technician nor a scientist, which reward system should you try to use-the economic reward system or more symbolic scientific reward system (recognition for papers, etc.) (Barnes, 1985)? Credibility with the user community and the MRC were both important for the survival of the organisation and the Centre's commitments to each were obviously inter-twined. Fulfilling the remit of the Centre should, in most cases, have fulfilled both sets of commitments as an efficient, fully automated service would have also contributed to the mission for which the money was awarded. Nevertheless, there was a formal line of accountability from the Resource Centre to the MRC, via the Resource Centre Steering Group and the PMC. Lines of accountability to the user community were much less clear. Related to this issue is the somewhat obvious albeit important, point that the MRC had more power in the short term to affect the survival of the Centre than did its client community.

Accreditation for the skills of the Resource Centre did not generally come through playing the scientific game. Or, in more theoretical terms, through joining the scientific 'cycle of credibility' (Latour & Woolgar, 1979). There was no obligation for Resource Centre users to acknowledge the services of the Centre in their publications. The Resource Centre itself does not publish to any great extent. A search of the Science Citation Index for the period from January 1990 to October 1993 showed four papers with members of the Centre as joint authors:

three of the papers were on computing aspects of the project (Rysavy, 1992; Rysavy *et al.*, 1992) and one was on gene mapping (Kunz *et al.*, 1993). A possible disincentive could have been that publishing or co-authoring might have compromised the neutrality of the Centre as a repository of information. In practice, institutional credibility with the user community has been acknowledged through more informal means, such as the fact that the Centre has over a thousand registered users, shop-window open days for industry, plus the overwhelmingly positive comments made about the service in a 1992 user survey (Bates, 1992). The reactions of the user community, moreover, were quite likely to feed back into the deliberations of the Cell Board through word of mouth and other informal means.

It has been far easier - if not imperative - for the Centre to justify its existence in economic terms, rather than through scientific or bibliometric indicators. As institutional arrangements demand ever increasing accountability from science, it has been easier to justify its existence with 1980s-style management yardsticks. Hence, the Project Manager's statement that the "guiding principle in deciding what should be done at the Resource Centre - and how much of the total budget of the Project should be committed to it - is *value-for-money*" (emphasis added) (Vickers, 1991a). Elsewhere, the Project Manager referred to this measure as a properly 1980s Whitehall one which had been used within the civil service (MRC, 1992). In fact, when the MRC reviewed the Resource Centre in 1992-3, the review subcommittee took up the civil service approach and broke value-for-money into three categories of economy, effectiveness and efficiency. The 'factory of the future' analogy tends to reinforce the notion that such yardsticks, rather than publication counts or other indicators, may be appropriate for this type of work.

Placement of the Resource Centre largely within the economic reward system, rather than the scientific reward system, was partly deliberate. Specific choices, such as to eschew a full research programme, facilitated this arrangement. On the other hand, the eventual position of the Centre in the science system was also a reflection of broader trends in accountability as the Resource Centre came under continual scrutiny by the MRC wishing to see how its administrative experiment turned out. The MRC in turn was responding to a government who wished to see value-for-money (efficiency) built into the public sector (Edgerton & Hughes, 1989; Sharp & Walker, 1990).

## The HGMP after 1991

For the sake of completeness, it is worth noting a number of other developments in HGMP policy that occurred during its initial 3 years. They will not be analysed in detail as they occurred after the majority of interviews had been performed for the case study. At the end of March 1992 the initial 3-year period of funding for the HGMP expired. The project continued in its existing form with £4.5 million being assimilated into the baseline of the MRC, which meant that the MRC was not no longer obliged to earmark the sum for genome mapping. It had also been made clear to the genome community that the protected nature of the project would eventually be dismantled (Rees, 1992; Vickers, 1991b, 1992). At the end of 1992 the entire project was subjected to a review, justified as a part of the normal MRC procedures for assessing its research institutes (Rees, 1992). A subcommittee of nine scientists, two from overseas, was established to undertake the review. The process included site visits to the Resource Centre and peer reviews from 17 referees.

As a result of the review the DPC and PMC were replaced by a single Coordinating Committee and the formulation of UK strategies was made the responsibility of Research Development Groups. Grant applications were to be peer reviewed by the MRC's replacement for the Cell Board, the Molecular and Cellular Medicine Board. The Resource Centre was also relocated to a Cambridge site adjacent to the Sanger Centre for genome research and the European Bioinformatics Institute. The move took place in 1994.

## Conclusion

It has been argued that the HGMP Resource Centre cannot be adequately characterised a part of the division of intellectual and manual labour prevalent in post-1945 science, the age of science policy (Gummett, 1991; Freeman, 1991). New modes of supporting and organising research, epitomised by the HGMP as a directed and mission-oriented programme, have helped to create a unique role for the Research Centre in the science system. As mentioned, a new type of scientific centre and a novel category of worker have emerged in molecular biology. This, in turn, generates problems related to institutional accreditation and also for the individual employees. The latter in terms of both individual reward and future career directions.

At a broader level, a single case study on its own cannot verify the arguments of Crook *et al.* and Gibbons *et al.* (Platt, 1988). It can, however, serve qualitatively to illustrate the changes about which the authors have theorised. To the extent that the HGMP may be representative of the future of science policy, it appears that the Centre and its work can be regarded as a new site and mode of knowledge production within molecular biology. It remains to be seen, nevertheless, whether these modes of work established in the HGMP last longer than its initial setting-up phase and whether the semi-centralised model is adopted more widely; or, alternatively, whether the Resource Centre is a unique and transient phenomenon in the organisation and management of science.

## Acknowledgements

I would like to thank all of the scientists and policy-makers who agreed to be interviewed in the course of this research. I am particularly grateful to Dr Tony Vickers for his assistance and comments on an earlier version of this paper.

## References

Alwen, J. (1990) United Kingdom Human Genome Mapping Project: background, development, components, coordination and management, and international links of the project. *Genomics*, **6**, 386-388.

Balmer, B. (1993) Mutations in the Research System? The Human Genome Mapping Project as Science Policy. Unpublished DPhil Thesis, University of Sussex, Brighton.

Baltimore, D. (1987) Genome sequencing: a small science approach. *Issues in Science and Technology*, **3**, 48-50.

Barnes, B. (1985) *About Science*. Blackwell, Oxford.

Bates, C. (1992) *A Report on the Quantitative Survey of Registered Users of the HGMP Resource Centre*, Unpublished Report, HGMP Resource Centre, Harrow.

Braun, D. (1993) Biomedical research in a period of scarcity: the United States and Great Britain. *Minerva*, **31**, 268-290.

Collins, H.M. (1985) *Changing Order*. Sage, London.

Crook, S., Pakulski, J. & Waters, M. (1992) *Post-modernisation: Change in Advanced Society*. Sage, London.

Davis, B.D. (1990) Human Genome Project-is big science bad for biology-yes-it bureaucratises, politicises research. *The Scientist*, **4**, 13.

Edgerton, D. & Hughes, K. (1989) The poverty of science: a critical analysis of scientific and industrial policy under Mrs Thatcher. *Public Administration*, **67**, 419-433.

Freeman, C. (1991) Grounds for hope: technology, progress and the quality of life. *Science and Public Policy*, **18**, 407-418.

Fujimura, J.H. (1988) The molecular biological bandwagon in cancer research: where social worlds meet. *Social Problems*, **35**, 261-283.

Galloway, J. (1990) Britain and the human genome. *New Scientist*, **127**, 41-46.

Gibbons, M., Limoges, C., Nowotny, H., Schwartzman, S., Scott, P & Trow, M. (1994). *The New Production of Knowledge: The Dynamics of Science and Research in Contemporary Societies*. Sage, London.

Gummett, P. (1991) The evolution of science and technology policy: a UK perspective. *Science and Public Policy*, **18**, 31-37.

Jordan, K. & Lynch, M. (1993) The mainstreaming of a molecular biological tool: a case study of a new technique. In Button, G. (ed). *Technology in Working Order: Studies in Work, Interaction and Technology*. Routledge, London, 162-178.

Knorr-Cetina, K.D. (1981) *The Manufacture of Knowledge: An Essay on the Constructivist and Contextual Nature of Science*. Pergamon Press, Oxford.

Kunz, J., Speich, N., Scherer, S., Kalffsuske, M., Du, Y.Z., Elaswrapu, R., Tsui, L.L. & Grzescik, K.A. (1993) Physical mapping of chromosome 7. *American Journal of Human Genetics*, **53**, 1317.

Latour, B. & Woolgar, S. (1979) *Laboratory Life: The Social Construction of Scientific Facts*. Sage, London.

MRC (1991) *The UK Human Genome Mapping Project*. Project Manager's Report. Medical Research Council, London.

MRC (1992) *MRC Review of the UK Human Genome Mapping Project*. Project Manager's Report, Medical Research Council, London.

Parsons, J.D., Brenner, S. & Bishop, M.J. (1992) Clustering cDNA sequences. *Computer Applications in the Biosciences*, **8**, 461-466.

Platt, J. (1988) What can case studies do? *Studies in Qualitative Methodology*, **1**, 1-23.

Rees, D.A. (1992) The future of the UK Human Genome Mapping Project. *G-Nome News*, **12**, 4-5.

Rysavy, F.R. (1992) Users and providers-interoperability. *Computer Networks and ISDN Systems*, **25**, 339-343.

Rysavy, F.R., Bishop, M.J., Gibbs, G.P. & Williams, G.W. (1992) The UK Human Genome Mapping Project Online Computer Service. *Computer Applications in the Biosciences*, **8**, 149-154.

Senker, P. (1992) Automation and work in Britain. In Adler, P.S. (ed) *Technology and the Future of Work*. Oxford University Press, Oxford, 89-110.

Senker, P. & Beesley, M. (1986) The need for skills in the factory of the future. *New Technology, Work and Employment*, **1**, 9-17.

Shapin, S. (1989) The invisible technician. *American Scientist*, **77**, 554-563.

Sharp, M. & Walker, W. (1990) Thatcherism and technical advance: reform without progress? *The Political Quaterly*, **62**, 262-272, 318-337.

Smith, R. (1988a) Peering into the bowels of the MRC I: setting priorities. *British Medical Journal*, **296**, 484-488.

Smith, R. (1988b) Peering into the bowels of the MRC II: review systems. *British Medical Journal*, **296**, 556-560.

Vickers, T. (1990) HGMP Resource Centre. *G-Nome News*, **5**, 4-6.

Vickers, T. (1991a) The Resource Centre of the UK Human Genome Mapping Project. *MRC News*, **53**, 52.

Vickers, T. (1991b) HGMP update, *G-Nome News*, **7**, 6-7.

Vickers, T. (1992) HGMP and Resource Centre update. *G-Nome News*, **11**, 3-4.

Wilkie, T. (1993) Perilous Knowledge: The Human Genome Project and Its Implications. Faber and Faber, London.

Ziman, J. (1987) *Science in a Steady State: The Research System in Transition.* SPSG, London.

# 3 How Weak Bonds Stick? Genetic Diagnosis Between the Laboratory and the Clinic

JEAN-PAUL GAUDILLIÈRE

ABSTRACT     *Medical genetics was a low-ranked speciality in France until the late 1980s. A few technologies could be mobilised to evaluate genetic risk and conduct counselling sessions. Chromosome analysis and statistical surveys of defects in newborns were combined with routine clinical examination. Although medical geneticists were usually pediatricians, they were viewed by many clinicians acting in the wards as resources that could be employed to manage the uncertainty and failure of clinical work and cope with the anxiety of families. The spreading of tools and instruments developed by molecular biologists as well as the establishment of large research programmes on the analysis of the human genome have triggered important changes. Medical genetics is now viewed by the general public as a highly scientific and promising field, Polymerise chain reaction (PCR) kits, DNA probes or sequencing machines are elements of a new form of life which complement the description of symptoms and the analysis of pedigrees. Specialists in oncology, haematology, cardiology, etc. are eager to launch collaborations with medical geneticists. This chapter will address these changes by focusing on one setting, the medical genetics department of a sick children's hospital in a French metropolis. It will discuss the local courses of actions which combine genotypes and symptoms, narrow diagnostic uncertainties, and stabilise the bonds between genetic research and medical work.*

## Introduction

In 1988, in the early days of the new human genome research, a group of French molecular biologists headed by Daniel Cohen and Jean Dausset sent the European Community a proposal to organise a systematic effort to map the human genome. The programme focused on the medical applications of DNA probes of known position: a complete set of genetic markers would facilitate the identification of genes which make individuals prone to specific diseases. This attempt at defining predictive medicine aroused strong criticism in the European Parliament. Finally, the project was modified to focus on the development of mapping procedures. At the same time, however, predictive medicine was becoming an important aspect of the American human genome initiative. As molecular biologist L. Hood (1994) once wrote:

> Perhaps in twenty years it will be possible to take DNA from newborns and analyse fifty or more genes for the allelic forms that can predispose the infant to many common diseases - cardiovascular, cancer, autoimmune, or metabolic. For each defective gene there will be therapeutic regimes that will circumvent the limitations of the defective gene. Thus medicine will move from a reactive mode (curing sick patients) to a preventive mode (keeping people well). Preventive medicine should enable most individuals to live a normal, healthy, and intellectually alert life without disease.

Social scientists and critical biologists often stress the limitations and vagueness of the prospects associated with medical genetics. They usually consider predictive medicine as a political tool which was instrumental in securing funds for human genome research. Since genetic predisposition is very complex, the bonds between genotype and pathological phenotypes will prove too fragile to result in the prediction of multifactorial diseases and specific courses of medical action. Accordingly, the jurisdiction of molecular medicine will remain within the boundaries defined by the study of these hereditary defects which are known to be caused by mutations in one or a few genes.

In contrast to this biological and political assessment, the recent development of breast cancer genetics suggests that predictive medicine is not only a promise but a trend rooted in weak bonds between laboratory practices and medical work which characterise the development of genetic diagnosis. This paper analyses some of the social and cognitive processes which make these weak bonds stick.

## Molecular Genetics in a Paediatric Hospital

In 1983, the medical anthropologist Charles Bosk introduced his book on genetic counselling in a paediatric hospital in an attempt to explain why he had been invited to observe the relationship between geneticists, physicians and patients (Bosk, 1992). His point was that medical geneticists had been eager to share with an outsider the burden of dealing with medical uncertainty, genetic risk and death. Genetic counselling within the paediatric hospital was a very special activity. Geneticists did not treat individuals, they advised families. They did not care for existing patients but discussed the fate of fetuses and future generations. This was an anxious community trying to put genetic risks under control while coping with powerlessness and uncertainty. Bosk's genetic counsellors did not make clinical decisions and the profession ranked poorly within the hospital hierarchy. They were usually called on the ward following the death of an infant, and their work was highly dependent on the goodwill and agenda of local pediatricians.

A decade later, medical genetics seems to be quite a different world. Reports in scientific journals and popular periodicals describe a profession working at the cutting edge of biomedical research. Medical geneticists are portrayed as key players in human genome research who translate laboratory tools invented by molecular biologists into medical innovations. Thus, the evaluation of risk is no longer empirical practice but the measurement of probabilities based on the knowledge of specific changes in the DNA structure. Although reproductive choices remain the current outcome of counselling sessions following pre-natal diagnosis, post-natal diagnosis or risk evaluation, genetic therapy is a promising area of research. Not surprisingly, this scientific credibility has triggered medical prestige. In many research hospitals, clinicians who were once reluctant are eager to collaborate with newly staffed genetic services.

Beyond the headlines, however, work in a medical genetic service remains life in uncertainty. One may think that activities have become more complex and fragile because the aim is to combine two different social worlds: the research laboratory and the clinical ward. In order to discuss this conjunction and the management of local uncertainties, I will focus on the work organisation and work practices observed in a department of medical genetics located in a children's hospital in a French metropolis (names and local circumstances have been altered to preserve the confidentiality of inter-viewees). The service was established as a department of *génétique pédiatrique* in post-war France. In the early 1960s, a research unit was established by the state agency for medical research and it became a reference centre for chromosomal analysis and genetic diagnosis. In the late 1980s, the development of an integrated unit which includes a research laboratory, an outpatient service for genetic counselling and a service centre doing routine molecular diagnosis was facilitated by state and private initiatives for the advancement of human genome research. In particular, the French muscular dystrophy association - the Association Française contre les Myopathies (AFM) - played an important role in the development of genetic research at the children's hospital.

In 1986, while American molecular biologists articulated the idea of a global attack on the sequencing of the human genome, Dr Bernard, then professor of medical genetics at the children's hospital, convinced two scientists in his laboratory to launch linkage analysis with the aim of developing chromosomal markers. In 1987, the AFM imported Telethon - the American TV-based fund-raising campaign - in France. The first trial at presenting muscular dystrophy to a wide popular audience resulted in a huge collection of FF 200 million. This success transformed a small-scale support association into a major patron of French biomedical research. The AFM 1988 research budget (roughly FF 160 million) compared favourably with the funds allocated by large charities (see Pinell, 1992) such as the Association pour la Recherche sur le Cancer (ACR). (Between 1980 and 1987, the ARC collected roughly FF 150 million per year for French biomedical laboratories). The AFM had been established with the mediation of a core set of biomedical researchers (Paterson & Barral, 1994). Telethon provided the means to modify this relationship between the organisation and the French specialists of (hereditary) neuromuscular disorders. Under the lead of a retired electrical engineer whose son died from Duchenne muscular dystrophy, the AFM set up a new research policy which focused on genetics. A three-stage programme emerged: firstly, create a mapping infrastructure and develop sequencing tools, secondly, identify the mutated genes causing muscular disorders and other hereditary defects; thirdly, invent the procedures for gene therapy (Barataud, 1992). Following debates between AFM officials and D. Cohen from the Centre d'Etudes du Polymorphisme Humain (CEPH) - a privately funded research centre which had been established to investigate the correlations between special sets of histocompatibility markers and chronic diseases such as diabetes, myocardial infraction or atherosclerosis - special emphasis was placed on systematic mapping of the entire human genome. The decision was made to implement this project within the framework of a new AFM centre for genetic research-Genethon-which would be built in a Paris suburb (Cohen, 1993). (It should be mentioned that the mapping project was not invented by the AFM:CEPH scientists were already discussing the issue with Collaborative Researchers and other players in the American HGP). Beside this commitment to large-scale and centralised research, the AFM supported a large number of local programmes. Muscular disorders were supplemented with a wide range of genetic disorders and by 1990 the fund-raising campaign was run under the claim that the AFM goal was to win the war against genetic disorders.

One important target in the AFM strategy was spinal muscular atrophy (SMA). Families with a child suffering from chronic forms of the disease belonged to the nucleus of the organisation. According to François, a neuropediatrician at the children's hospital:

> Within AFM there was a group of parents and children who strongly felt (they were) superior. In contrast to many children affected with muscular dystrophy, kids affected with spinal muscular atrophy do not show mental retardation or sensory loss. Intelligence is often above average. Thus, there is a hierarchy of neuromuscular handicaps. At the top of AFM, one could find SMA families.

In 1987, the first research project concerned with the identification of putative pathological genes which was supported by the AFM with Telethon funds focused on SMA. The DMD gene involved in the Duchenne type muscular dystrophy had been cloned in 1986 and scientific advisors quite naturally advocated an analogous strategy. The genetic service at the children's hospital had no specific credential in localisation studies but it won the contract. As Marc, a senior researcher at the children's hospital, put it:

> The head of the lab - Dr Bernard - told the AFM people that he could establish a genetic laboratory in a paediatric hospital. There was a meeting of the scientific board and Bernard said he could do it. An influential person in French genetics had sent a letter and proposed to identify the gene. But he couldn't attend the meeting. Thus Bernard said that he would do it if only AFM could help establish a new lab. Bernard was sitting on the AFM scientific board. They had been impressed with his authority and political awareness.

By the spring of 1988, the association allocated funds for the cost of equipping a laboratory of molecular genetics which would be closely linked to the paediatric genetic service. In addition to the SMA research contract, AFM fellowships supported researchers working on smaller projects such as studies of malformations or mitochondrial diseases.

SMA work was to be completed under the leadership of a molecular biologist experienced in chromosomal analysis and cellular hybridisation who had run the first mapping project. The obvious strategy consisted in the search for a significant correlation between the transmission of the disease within affected families and the transmission of genetic markers of known position.

The project depended upon the collection of three major resources: DNA samples from patients diagnosed with SMA and from their relatives, restriction fragment-linked polymorphism (RFLP) probes recognising specific polymorphic segments of the human genome and statistical tools for linkage analysis. Collaboration with CEPH scientists would facilitate the domestication of probes and softwares. Collaboration with neuropediatricians was necessary to recruit the families. The molecular biologist heading the project failed to establish this medical network: after a few months the SMA team was still waiting for a significant number of DNA samples. Informal pressure from the AFM increased and by the end of an internal reshuffling of responsibilities. The assistant in medical genetics, Dr Laurent - then head of a team studying metabolic diseases at the enzymatic and DNA levels - proposed to take over the SMA project with a group comprising a young neuropediatrician with laboratory training and a few technicians. By the same token, Laurent reinforced his position as a putative director of the genetic service. One year later, Dr Bernard's retirement and a professorship in medical genetic brought these personnel changes to an end.

## Genetic Diagnosis: Clinical or Molecular?

A department where people provided genetic counsel while investigating the classification and modes of transmission of genetic disorders was transformed into a centre which combined medical activities and heterogeneous laboratory studies ranging from biochemical analysis to computerised linkage analysis or DNA sequencing. Thus, genetic diagnosis has become part of two different worlds. On the one hand, it is linked to the routine assessment of patients referred to the genetic service. On the other hand, it is a preliminary stage in the description of molecular analysis of pathologies.

Consequently, one may be tempted to argue that routine diagnosis and research diagnosis pertain to different professions. Usually, they are not accomplished by medical geneticists and molecular geneticists who differ in training, work habits, skills, interests and visions of human genetics. Thus, one could speak of a 'knowledge transfer' problem, i.e. the fact that clinical experience may not be translated into biological wisdom and vice versa. Once identified, this knowledge transfer problem could be interpreted as a sociological problem dealing either with communication issues or with institutional entrenchments. A (medical) sociological explanation of how people combine genotypes and phenotypes, MDs and PhDs, laboratories and hospital wards should therefore consist of an analysis of professional roles. In contrast, our field work at the children's hospital suggest that it is increasingly less probable that the division of labour opposing genetic counselling and molecular genetics will be a matter of professional organisation. This is not to say that boundaries between the clinical and the biological simply disappear but to suggest that they might be better understood in terms of contrasting case trajectories. Two examples will introduce 'routine' and 'fascinoma' trajectories as different biomedical procedures.

The example of 'routine trajectory' starts with the arrival of a blood sample in the genetic service section which carries out DNA analysis for the clinical departments at the children's hospital. The form accompanying the test-tube recalls that it has been sent for the detection of mutations in the cystic fibrosis gene. Previously, a phone call warned the medical geneticist that it is a case of ileus meconial. Soon standard studies with several DNA probes show that one gene has a well-known mutation called delta-F508. The probes available do not identify a second mutation. The situation is unclear. Either the child has one single mutation or the detection system used by the geneticist failed for contingent or methodological reasons. The child may be a 'true' heterozygous who is not affected with cystic fibrosis. Alternatively, the child may be a real case of cystic fibrosis who is a 'complex' heterozygous showing two mutations. A decision has to be made quickly. A short discussion between the geneticist and the clinician in charges settles the matter: on the basis of clinical evidence, it is a cystic fibrosis case. No further analysis is attempted although a new blood sample could have been taken and sent to the national reference laboratory for cystic fibrosis.

The outcome of routine diagnosis is a counselling session either with the family or with the referring clinician. From the geneticist viewpoint, the procedure starts with an 'index case' - often an affected child. Assessment of the medical demands is an unspoken prerequisite: what does the family, the general practitioner or the referring paediatrician think? What are their expectations? Formal options then consist of the establishment of a presumptive diagnosis from the clinical data and the prescription of laboratory investigations. The final diagnosis may be specific or not. It may or may not include a prognosis and figures for the recurrence. Whatever the nature of the final evaluation, a routine diagnosis is defined by the fact that unexpected events and uncertainties do not generate a problem: the geneticist's work terminates with the(last) counselling session and records are archived. This does not imply that a routine trajectory is an easy path, it just means that issues are handled on the basis of existing knowledge and established work habits.

Our example of 'fascinoma trajectory' starts with a phone call reaching the same geneticist experienced in the diagnosis and care of metabolic disorders. A clinician on duty in the intensive care unit at a neighbouring hospital 'received' a child showing acute hypoglycaemia and confusing heart problems. Following a short discussion of symptoms and biochemical results, the geneticist offers a diagnosis - it is a defect of an enzyme involved in the breakdown of fats - and care advice. The boy survives. Later, the family is recruited by the geneticist. Clinical examination and sampling at the genetic service provides the material for a biochemical and genetic study.

A fascinoma trajectory may start with routine demands but at some point in the investigative path uncertainties regarding the clinical status or the biological data are transformed into an 'interesting' abnormality. Then, the procedure is centred on the collection of resources which are necessary to design a 'do-able problem': previously published clinical cases, instruments, embodied skills, medical samples (Fujimura, 1987). The normal outcome is the creation of a typical biomedical pattern through the on-going investigation of genotypes based on changing tools. While fascinoma trajectories were, until the late 1970's merely epidemiological and statistical, they have become increasingly based on 'instrumentalities' originating in the human genome projects, i.e. RFLP markers, microsatellites, YACs, contigs, DNA sequences, gene sequence databases, and so forth. Finally, fasinoma trajectories establish new responses for case management.

In her analysis of brain research in the nineteenth century, the sociologist of science S. Leigh Star (1983) distributed local uncertainties of scientific work into four classes: taxonomic uncertainties, diagnostic uncertainties, technical uncertainties and political uncertainties. In like manner, one may divide uncertainties in the practice of genetic diagnosis into three classes: clinical uncertainty, molecular uncertainty and prognosis uncertainty. (Table 1). Clinical uncertainty pertains to the medical work preceding the articulation of research problems. For instance, workable pedigrees may be difficult to obtain during counselling sessions. One current response is to enrol several relatives. Medical records may not be reliable and previous examination may raise doubts. Taxonomic uncertainty focuses on problems that must be handled by referring to professional classification schemes. Hence, a complex use of databanks, published cases and exemplars. Finally, recurrent problems originate in the rarity of 'interesting' cases . As a large number of 'abnormalities' emerge as isolated clinical demands, they are not going to be researched in the near future. One decisive step towards a 'do-able' problem is the establishment of a medical network for recruiting patients diagnosed with similar pathologies. The division of clinical work, the increasing role of 'reference centres' for one genetic disease or the recruitment by patient organisation are important elements in this process.

Molecular uncertainty underlies statements that specific defects in DNA structure cause the disease to run in a given family. Tools used by molecular biologists working in a medical context consist of polymerise chain reaction (PCR) kits, sequencing machines, primer and marker sequences stored in databanks, oligonucleotide synthesising machines, and so forth. Molecular uncertainty relates to the skills required to operate these instruments properly. A general response to molecular uncertainty is therefore to enforce the standardisation of materials and work practices within the local setting. In contrast, uncertainty about the interpretation of molecular analysis is handled at the public level. It is widely acknowledged that there are no universal 'standards' for what is good evidence for a molecular cause. Theoretical standards are therefore replaced by practical standards which define acceptable results. For example, doubts may be ruled out with an increasing number of 'controls' such as non affected individuals who do not show the suspected mutation. A few dozen controls may be sufficient, but public disagreement may increase the norm.

Table 1. Local uncertainties and genetic diagnosis

|  | Issues | Responses |
|---|---|---|
| Clinical uncertainty | Rarity of cases | Organise Medical network |
|  | Pedigree difficult to obtain | Mobilise relatives |
|  | Incomplete examination | Replicate and search for other methods |
|  | False results of tests |  |
|  | Labile symptoms | Uses of exemplars and/or medification of taxonomy |
|  | Incompetent clinicians or staff | Segmentation of work and training |
| Molecular uncertainty | Uncontrollable procedures | Standardise reagents and protocols during workshops, organise blind tests |
|  | Mapping or sequencing errors | Division of labour, exchange materials, combine old and new procedures, unify mapping tools |
|  | Meaningless mutation, polymorphism | Search for analogies in databases, run high number of controls, substitute biological plausibility for technical consistency |
| Prognostic uncertainty | Hazardous linkage between genetic markers and disease Variability of expression, low penetration | Use statistical models of errors, expand the size of the family pool Segment the targeted population |
|  | Low compliance of patients and unknown psychsocial effects | Organise psychological counselling, complete cost-benefit analysis |

Prognosis uncertainty is the most widely discussed. Not least because it bears upon the use of complex genotype/phenotype relationships within the context of counselling. Once identified, a mutation may be simple polymorphism, it may result in little changes of the protein, it may be neutralised by duplicated genes, the metabolic deficiency may be compensated at the cellular level, and so forth. In practice, prognosis uncertainty means that biologists and clinicians work out a formula linking a set of molecular data and the natural history of a pathology. Obvious discrepancies may be handled by changing nosological entities. For instance, specific prognosis may be facilitated by splitting the medical population. Alternatively, intractable variability may be expressed at the theoretical level with concepts such as 'low penetrance' which summarises statistical knowledge of cases showing a molecular defect without clinical symptoms. When dealing with patients or families, probabilistic assessments arouse a series of unknown consequences. Current responses include sociological studies and psychological counselling.

## The SMA Consortium: Clinical Regress and Regulated Order

In order to illustrate the integrative management of uncertainties associated with routine and fascinoma diagnosis, I will focus on certain aspects of the SMA study launched at the children's hospital. In January 1990, international research on SMA entered a new phase with the mapping of a candidate region on chromosome 5 by an Anglo-American consortium. At the children's hospital, this was especially bad news since work was just gathering momentum. Problems related to the recruitment of SMA patients and the collection of genetic markers are worth mentioning.

Firstly, a limited circulation of genetic markers was circumvented by the circulation of people. In 1988, only a few RFLPs were available. DNA probes were obtained from CEPH in the US and their chromosomal location was investigated at the children's hospital. The pace of the work was accelerated by the use of probes originating in Y. Nakamura's laboratory but systematic survey of the genome seemed to be out of order for a long time: for every chromosome only five to ten polymorphic markers were known. By the late 1988, rumour had it that Ray White had generated a larger series and computed their informativity. One team in Paris was already using this series. Negotiations to get them circulated achieved nothing. Thus, the scientists in charge of the SMA project spent a few days in White's laboratory at Salt Lake City duplicating his probes. This was how they got started.

Secondly, a 'French Spinal Muscular Atrophy Investigators' network emerged from the mobilisation of the AFM support group. Collaboration with pediatricians, neuropediatricians and geneticists involved in the care of SMA patients in France was formally established by the new head of the project. Letters requesting clinical histories, pedigree information and blood samples from families with SMA were sent to relevant specialists. The neuropaediatrician leading the research started to visit clinical services all over the country in order to urge the physicians to participate and to collect samples and records. In early 1989, however, a large-scale collection was organised by the SMA support group set up within the framework of the AFM. French neuropediatricians resented this campaign as the emergence of an alternative power. The collection was a one-day event gathering all the members in the support group. Pedigree information and blood were collected by 'commissioned' researchers. Physicians in charge were not informed and diagnoses were not cross-checked. As one informant told us:

> The Dourdan collection was the first time AFM self-managed a research operation. Then they realised how powerful they were ... For the first time we got the feeling that a power alternative to the hospital and the clinicians was emerging. Medicine was debarred, eliminated. They were speaking of taking destiny back into their hands, of empowerment. Two worlds facing each other. With respect to our practice, there was a major problem: self-help and identity were forming the basis of diagnosis. No paediatrician, so semiology, no examination. Nosological analysis? We don't care. That was the beginning of a long process which resulted in absurd public collection campaigns with 1-800 numbers.

The 'counter move' was to reinforce the collaboration between neuropediatricians and SMA specialists. One outcome was a gathering which suggested 'homogeneous' criteria for entry into the genetic study. This study was based on the definition of 'true' SMA accepted by the majority of clinicians, i.e. Dubowitz's review of SMA classifications:

> SMA were selected on the following diagnostic criteria: (i) proximal, symmetrical limb and trunk weakness; (ii) muscle atrophy without facial or extraocular involvement; (iii) no spasticity, hyperreflexia, sensory loss or mental retardation; (iv) electromyographic studies showing enervation and diminished motor action potential amplitude with normal or slow nerve conduction velocities; and (v) muscle biopsy consistent with enervation with no evidence of storage material or other structural abnormalities.

Classification of families into subgroups was done by the researchers at the children's hospital.

Early in December 1989, the French team had already excluded three-quarters of the human genome when the rumour circulated that the Ango-American consortium had mapped an SMA gene. Although the French workers managed to confirm the putative location a few weeks later, the game seemed to be over. (There were tense priority debates at that time, but these will not be discussed here.) The work and resources invested in the collection of markers as well as numerous informative families was of no direct benefit to further research since the knowledge of flanking marker sequences would provide any geneticist with the opportunity of participating in the chromosomal walk which would lead to a precise identification of candidate genes. Yet, a possibility to cash in on the building of the medical network, the large pool of recruited families, and the collection of markers was to focus on the clinical diversity of SMAs. Reports on genetic homogeneity triggered a typical 'clinical regress' debate.

Clinical regress is a notion which is helpful in analysing a situation akin to the process of experimenter's regress described by the sociologist H. Collins (1985). Similarities stem from the fact that the establishment of correlations between biological genotypes and medical phenotypes depends upon an agreed nosology which in turn may change according to biological data. In other words, the search for genes causing SMAs required that a set of methodological and factual issues be addressed at the same time. Are the different forms of SMA one or several diseases? Is each form of SMA caused by one or by several genes? Are the patient pools representative? Are the biological assays reliable? Clinical regress specifically pertains to uncertainty of the medical importance of the work done by molecular biologists. Conclusions regarding the genetic identity of SMA were thus based on tacit assumptions on the classification of patients and the clinical identity of the disease. Clinicians may not use the same criteria to define what a 'true' SMA is whether they think that severe and mild forms are different pathological entities or different presentations of one single disease. Similarly, researchers may consider genetic homogeneity within a small set of SMA patients either as typical of the general population or as an artefact reflecting classification and recruitment problems. Similar debates focusing on the mutual definition of 'true' syphilis and good serological assays have been described (Fleck, 1979).

SMA clinical regress became apparent following the publication of reports on the localisation of genes involved in severe forms of the disease. With a handful of families as samples, the first article by the Ango-American consortium argued for the location of a gene for chronic SMA diagnosed in childhood but did not announce decisive evidence for the acute form with onset in early infancy. The authors recalled that "a maximum log likelihood ratio (lod score) of three or more is appropriate for declaring linkage" and the figures they obtained with "six families, diagnosed with acute SMA" peaked at 1.6 (Brzustowicz *et al.*, 1990). A few weeks later, four consanguineous families had been collected and included in the study. Lod score computation showed that the genetic markers used to define the location of the gene for seven chronic SMA families peaked at 13 when two families were excluded. The message was "genetic homogeneity between acute and chronic forms of SMA" (Gilliam *et al.*, 1990). However, the two unlinked families raised "the possibility of genetic heterogeneity or disease misclassification among the SMA family set". The paper informally pointed to an alternative outcome to the attempts at matching biological and medical practices, genotype and phenotype. Either these and other families were viewed as affected with SMA and the disease was to be viewed as heterogeneous and caused by several genes, or clinical assessment would be altered - for the two families or more generally -and one single gene accounted for all forms of 'true' SMA. The French consortium added considerable credibility to the unifying perspective by analysing larger pools of SMA families: 25 families affected with acute (type 1) SMA and 39 families affected with chronic SMA (type II or III SMA) were 'informative'. Although the linkage situation with acute SMA remained disputable - lod score values of 2.36 were computed - values above 11 were obtained when all the families were analysed as one single class. Thus, "the hypothesis of heterogeneity was rejected" (Melki *et al.*, 1990).

This news was viewed as a mixed blessing. A *Lancet* editorial (1990) accompanying the publication of the French study commented that "linkage analysis was compatible with gene locus homogeneity between acute and chronic SMA". However, "there is some evidence of heterogeneity in the data, which suggests that a minority of families may have a mutation that does not map to the same locus". To the author of the editorial, this heterogeneity may 'create practical difficulties' until the time when the families in question were clinically or molecularly distinguishable. Meanwhile, "prenatal diagnosis and carrier detection on the basis of closely linked gene markers ... should probably be withheld from use in acute SMA for a short while until the question of heterogeneity is cleared up. This is not just pedantry but good medicine, because to make a prediction on the basis of an analysis of markers linked to the wrong gene will lead to errors, and errors in this sort of prenatal diagnosis have dire consequences." Thus, the research debate about nosological schemes and genetic heterogeneity was linked to clinical evaluation and practical issues in genetic counselling. A few weeks later, German geneticists emphasised the 'withholding' option. Arguing that "study of 234 cases from 206 families gives evidence that the condition may be heterogeneous", they raised several problems in SMA combining 'genetic heterogeneity' illustrated by the identification of cases with dominant or X-linked inheritance or 'atypical pedigrees' unexplained by simple autosomal recessive inheritance and 'misdiagnosis' exemplified by cases of Duchenne/Becker type progressive muscular dystrophy reported as chronic SMA (Serres *et al.*, 1990). The recommendation was there "that prenatal diagnosis with DNA markers should be withheld until the question of heterogeneity is clarified". Over the next 2 years the question of heterogeneity was not 'clarified' prior to prenatal diagnosis but 'rejected' on the basis of new nosological standards and new genetic counselling practices. Historical knowledge of SMA debates and the origins of the heterogeneity problems is required in order to comment on this outcome.

In 1991, the British neuropediatrician V. Dubowitz commented on the "chaos in classification of spinal muscular atrophies" with a historical survey. He argued that early clinical and genetic studies of SMA resulted in a decade long argument opposing lumpers and splitters (Dubowitz, 1991). Lumpers favoured genetic homogeneity and suggested there might be a continuum between severe infantile forms on the one hand and mildest distinct forms of SMA. Lumper and splitter debates are viewed by geneticists as two traditions or two 'thought styles' nutured by the uncertainty inherent in classification schemes based on conventional clinical practices rather than biological knowledge (McKusick, 1969). By contrast, I would like to suggest that the dynamics of post-war nosological debates on neuromuscular disorders was dominated by professional issues and genetic counselling practices.

Classification of muscular atrophies was a non-issue for almost 50 years following the description in the early 1890s by G. Werdnig and J. Hoffman of progressive muscle weakness attributed to atrophy of the anterior horm cell nerve cells and resulting in early death. Normal practice was clinical diagnosis based on symptoms including onset in enervation (Walton, 1956). The subject was complicated in the late 1950s as neurologists followed the analysis of E. Kugelberg and L. Welander in reclassifying cases of progressive muscular dystrophy as late onset and mild forms of SMA showing no mental or sensory disturbances, survival into adolescence and adulthood and motor neuronlesion under refined electromyography. Acute (Werdnig-Hoffman) and chronic (Kugelberg-Welander) then emerged as two clinical forms of a single 'heredofamilial recessive disorder'. Classification was merely a matter of age at onset and severity which determined the clinical fate, i.e. prognosis and provision for care. Thus as a young paediatrician in Sheffield, V. Dubowitz, argued that all grades of severity existed between "severe cases with weakness present at birth, early respiratory distress" and "patients with onset of mild weakness in infancy who remain ambulant and show little subsequent deterioration" (Dubowitz, 1964).

This pattern was altered in the 1960s following the rise of medical genetics and the establishment of genetic counselling services in paediatric hospitals. (There are few historical studies of genetic counselling. For the American case, see Terrenoir (1986).) SMAs became an interesting research topic for prominent human geneticists including A. Emery (Edinburgh), J. Pearn (London), V. McKusick (London) and P. Becker (Göttingen). The clinical continuum was then split into entities characterised by modes of transmission and medical courses. Late onset SMA revealed uncertain features with X-linked, autosomal dominant, late infantile, juvenile, adult, autosomal recessive forms characterised by heterogeneous risks. In contrast, acute and automosal recessive SMA became a stronghold for genetic counselling. Statistical surveys resulted in the attribution of 1:80 to 1:100 gene frequency and an almost predictable age of death. Genetic heterogeneity illustrated by variable classification schemes including 3, 4 or 7 SMA classes was reinforced by the existence of two forms of genetic management. On the one hand, variable chronic SMA was of uncertain prognosis, variable risk of recurrence and difficult care. On the other hand, homogeneous chronic SMA was of ascertained rapidly fatal course, 1:4 risk of recurrence and short-term care. The prevailing feeling among the genetic counsellors was that "unlike the more conservative approach of parents confronting chronic SMA, the objectively high risk of 1 in 4 is accepted in a surprisingly high percentage of cases" (Pearn, 1982).

By 1990, as opportunities for molecular diagnosis were envisioned, this linkage between norms of genetic counselling and the vision of an homogeneous acute SMA proved to be of decisive importance. Rather than being used to diagnose chronic SMA - which showed the clearest genetic linkage - DNA markers entered counselling sessions in the form of pre-natal diagnosis for couples who had already experienced the death of an acute SMA baby. Strong demands and clinical homogeneity balanced the risk of error. Pre-natal 'molecular' diagnosis was then advocated by both consortia and DNA markers started to circulate (Daniels *et al.*, 11992; Melki *et al.*, 1992). DNA markers were soon used to supplement the clinical diagnosis of chronic SMA. Finally, they provided the basis for presymptomatic diagnosis of chronic SMA (Brahe *et al.*, 1993). Confidence in the use of a single set of markers was reinforced by counselling experience: prognosis of safe babies proved right except in a very few instances which could be traced to 'misdiagnosis'.

This points to the fact that the consensus about genetic homogeneity would have been much more difficult to achieve if not for the collective regulation of nosological practices. In 1991, the Polish neuropaediatrician I. Hasmanowa-Petrusewicz (1991) once again argued for a classification dividing proximal

SMAs into five types. Based mainly on age of onset, course and bodily distribution, this classification included recessive and dominant modes of transmission. In addition, the scheme echoed genetic counselling concerns about heterogeneous empirical risks for chronic SMAs. Her conclusions resonated as a new word of caution targeted at molecular analysts:

> (1) Acute infantile SMA seems to be a unique disorder. (2) Autosomal recessive inheritance accounts for the vast majority of patients with chronic proximal SMA of childhood and adolescence. (3) Exceptions to autosomal recessive transmission see to occur in one group of chronic SMA cases. (4) The same mode of transmission does not necessarily mean a single gene. (5) Some data indicate that more than one gene is involved in chronic SMA. (6) It would be premature and unsubstantiated to express a categorical opinion about the number of forms of SMA on the basis of clinical evidence. (7) DNA linkage studies require the use of SMA pedigrees that have been selected by consistent criteria.

Her voice was, however, drowned out by members of the 'International SMA Collaboration'. In December 1990, this new consortium held its second meeting to define criteria for the diagnosis and classification of SMAs: "After considerable discussion, debate and compromise, consensus was achieved" (SMA, 1991). The streamlining of clinical practices aimed at producing "a framework for the molecular geneticist". On the one hand, exclusion criteria were reinforced: patients showing dysfunction of the central nervous system or other neurologic systems were excluded as well as patients with "involvement of other organs, i.e hearing, cardiac or vision". On the other hand, a simple classification was adopted to eliminate fine-tuned and skilled clinical assessment which was then viewed as too complex for achieving consistency in large-scale studies. For example, defining courses for type II (intermediate) SMA and type III (mild) SMA were 'never stand' and 'stands alone' respectively. With respect to the genetic heterogeneity question, this compromise achieved three goals. Firstly, the international consortium focused issues on autosomal recessive inheritance leaving out late onset dominant cases which had been troublesome (Kausch *et al.*, 1991). Secondly, the new criteria for inclusion were chosen in order to eliminate the families which did not conform to the chromosome 5 location in the French or the Ango-American study and reassessed as showing additional features such as cardiac abnormalities or cataract (*Lancet*, 1990). Thirdly, changes in nosological practices were complemented with a theoretical framework for handling abnormalities. In other words, the relationship between clinical features and results of DNA analysis became genotype/phenotype problems that were viewed in terms of variable expression of the SMA gene(s). Fourthly, the formal international collaboration stabilised a new hierarchy of SMA specialists with established neuropediatricians conceding authority to young molecular analysts advocating genetic homogeneity and clinical continuum.

## Conclusion

Further developments have shown that the 'black boxing' of genetic homogeneity was far from being the final word of SMA studies. (Different genes located within the targeted region of chromosome 5 have recently been attributed a decisive part in the causation of SMA by French and Canadian workers. This situation reopened the debate about the relationship between clinical variability and genetic causation.) This episode nonetheless highlights general features about the closure of clinical regress debates and the management of genetic uncertainty. Various responses to clinical, molecular and prognostic uncertainties were mobilised during the 1990-1991 debates: the use of exemplars, the standardisation of tools, the recruitment of new families, the segmentation of medical populations or the use of standardised statistical models. Two moves, however, were of special importance. Firstly, the negotiation of a new taxonomic order limited the variability of molecular analysis regarding the location and homogeneity of SMA genes. A nosological response provided a partial response to molecular uncertainty. Secondly, the circulation and use of a single set of DNA markers for acute and chronic SMA was facilitated by genetic counselling habits. Homogeneous prognostic practice thus provided an alternative to theoretical consistency. The clinical regress ended with the definition of new - and partly negotiated - norms for both SMA research activities and genetic counselling. Similar analysis of 'integrated regulatory work' in human genome research may well account for changes which have alternatively been viewed as cases of 'technological push', i.e. consequences of the spreading of sequencing machines, or as instances of 'social pull', i.e. the funding of research programmes by patient organisations.

## Acknowledgements

I gratefully acknowledge the willingness of interviewees to participate in this study and have their work observed and discussed by an outsider. I am indebted to H. Rothman and the participants in the workshop for comments and critiques.

## References

Barataud, B. (1992) *Au nom de nos enfants*. Editions n*1, Paris.

Bosk, C. (1992) *All God's Mistakes. Genetic Counselling in a Paediatric Hospital*. University of Chicago Press, Chicago.

Brahe, C., Zappata, S., Velona, I., Bertini, E., Servidei, S., Tonali, P. & Neri, G. (1993) Presymptomatic diagnosis of SMA III by genotype analysis. *American Journal of Medical Genetics*, **45**, 408-411.

Brzustowicz, L.M., Lehner, T., Castilla, L.H., Penchaszadeh, G.K., Willhelmsen, K.C., Daniels, R., Davies, K.E., Leppert, M., Ziter, F., Wood, D., Dubowitz, V., Zerres, K., Hausonanowa-Petrusewicz, I., Ott, J., Munsat, T.L. & Gilliam, T.C. (1990) Genetic mapping of chronic childhood-onset spinal muscular atrophy to chromosome 5q11.2-13.3. *Nature*, **344**, 540-541.

Cohen, D. (1993) *Les gènes de l'espoir. A la découverte du génome humain*. Robert Laffont, Paris.

Collins, H. (1985) *Changing Order: Replication and Induction in Scientific Practice*. Sage, London.

Daniels, R.J. Suthers, G.K., Morrison, K.E., Thomas, N.H., Francis, M.J., Mathew, C.G., Loughlin, S. (1992) Prenatal prediction of spinal muscular atrophy. *Journal of Medical Genetics*, **29**, 165-170.

Dubowitz, V. (1964) Infantile muscular atrophy: a prospective study with particular reference to a slowly progressive variety. *Brain*, **87**, 707-718.

Dubowitz, V. (1991) Chaos in classification of the spinal muscular atrophies of childhood. *Neuromuscular Disorders*, **1**, 77-80.

Fleck, L. (1979) *Genesis and Development of a Scientific Fact*. University of Chicago Press, Chigaco.

Fujimura, J. (1987) Constructing 'do-able' problems in cancer research: articulating alignment. *Social Studies of Science*, **17**, 257-293.

Gillian, T.C., Brzustowicz, L.M., Castilla, L.H., Lehner, T., Penchaszadeh, G.K., Daniels, R.J., Byth, B.C., Knowles, J., Hislop, J.E., Shapira, Y., Dubowitz, V., Munsat, T.L., Ott, J. & Davies, K.E. (1990) Genetic homogeneity between acute and chronic forms of spinal muscular atrophy. *Nature*, **345**, 823-825.

Hausmanowa-Petrusewicz, I. (1991) Spinal muscular atrophies: how many types? *Advances in Neurology*, **56**, 157-167.

Hood, L., (1994) Biology and medicine in the twenty-first century. In Kelves, D. & Hood, L. (eds) *The Code of Codes*. Harvard University Press, Cambridge, 158.

Kausch, K., Müller, C.R., Grimm, T., Richer, K., Rietschel, M., Rudnik-Schoneborn, S. & Zerres,K. (1991) No evidence for linkage of autosomal dominant proximal spinal muscular atrophies to chromosomes 5q makers. *Human Genetics*, **86**, 317-318.

Lancet (1990) Spinal muscular atrophies (editorial). *Lancet*, **336**, 280-281.

Leigh Star, S. (1983) Simplification in scientific work: an example from neuroscience research. *Social Studies of Science*, **13**, 205-228.

McKusick, V. (1969) On lumpers and splitters, or the nosology of genetic disease. *Perspectives in Biology and Medicine,* 298-312.

Melki, J., Sheth, P., Abdelhak, S., Birlet P., Bachelot, M.f., Lathrop, M.G., Frezal, J., Melki, J., Sheth, P., Abdelhak, S., Birlet, P., Rachin, V., Kaplan, J., Spiegel, R., Gilgenkrantz, S., Philip, N., Chauret, M.L., Dumez, Y. *et al.* (1992) Prenatal prediction of Werdnig-Hoffmann disease using linked polymorphic DNA probes. *Journal of Medical Genetics,* **29,** 171-174.

Munnich, A. & the French spinal muscular atrophy investigators (1990) Mapping of acute (type I) spinal muscular atrophy to chromosome 5q12-q14. *Lancet,* **336,** 271-273.

Paterson, F. & Barral, C. (1994) L'Asssosication Française contre les Myopathies: trajectoire d'une association d'usagers et construction associative d'une maladie. *Sciences Sociales et Santé,* **12,** 79-111.

Pearn, J., (1982) Infantile motor neuron disease. *Advances in Neurology,* **36,** 121-130.

Pinell, P., (1992) *La naissance d'un fléau.* A.M. Metailié, Paris.

Serres, K., Rudnik-Schöneborn, S. & Rietschel, M. (1990) Heterogeneity in proximal spinal muscular atrophy. *Lancet,* **336,** 749-750.

SMA (1991) Workshop Report International SMA collaboration. *Neuromuscular Disorder,* **1,** 81.

Terrenoire, G. (1986) L'évolution du conseil génétique aux Etats-Unis de 1940 á 1980: pratique et légitimation. *Sciences Sociales et Santé,* **4,** 51-79.

Walton, J.N. (1956) Amyotonia congenita. *Lancet,* 1023-1027.

# 4 Information Technology as an Instrument of Genetics

CHRISTINE HINE

ABSTRACT    This chapter describes an ethnographic study of the use of information technology (IT) in a laboratory engaged in research related to the Human Genome Project. The use of IT is portrayed as strategic, facultative and motivated. The role played by IT in narratives about work in the laboratory, about training needs and about discoveries is also strategic. It is suggested that this attitude towards IT, and the resulting invisibility of IT developers in the laboratory, contributes to the viewing of IT within the laboratory as just another scientific instrument, providing a transparent window on nature. This analysis draws on research in sociology and history of science about the role of instruments in scientific expertise, in discoveries, experiments, scientific organisation and research directions.

## Introduction

There are many places in which to site an interest in the implications of knowledge in human genetics. My interest is situated in the laboratory, in the construction of genetic knowledge, and the ways in which that knowledge comes to be. As we know, the laboratory and the scientific endeavour are inextricable tied up with the panoply of technologies which provide readings, traces and other inscriptions. These are the scientific instruments which provide for the enhancement of the scientists' senses, enabling them to see farther or nearer than their own eyes would allow them, and to distance themselves from involvement in their own observations. In the introduction to the collection *The Right Tools for the Job*, Clarke and Fujimura (1992) argue that tools, jobs and rightness are co-constructed: what comes to seem the right job for science to do, and the right tools with which to achieve it, are the upshot of processes of negotiation and 'articulation'. This suggests problems for a model of scientific progress which considers that particular directions are inevitable or obvious, the imperatives of current needs, technologies or questions, and it suggests that scientific progress

41

is not immune to influence from social concerns.  When the job to be done is the production of genetic knowledge about humans, it seems appropriate not just to study the impacts of this knowledge on society, but also to concern ourselves with the means by which this job, and the tools associated with it, come to be right.

Among the technologies which are implicated in human genome research are polymerise chain reaction (PCR), the automated gene sequencer, and the databases which store and analyse the accumulation of information.  My focus is on the last of these three, information technology (IT), without which all the accumulated knowledge would be a disorganised heap as unreadable as the genome itself.  I focus on IT as an instrument in order to highlight its role in the knowledge construction process, and to question the ways in which it fits into the laboratory.  I will concentrate on the ways in which the observer, the machine and the object of study are mutually constructed in laboratory discourse.  First, however, what is a scientific instrument, what roles have scientific experiments played in scientific knowledge construction, and what might be the purchase offered by treating IT as a scientific instrument?

## Scientific Instruments

### What Is a Scientific Instrument?

The term 'scientific instrument' may be taken in current terms, to mean a machine which provides data for use in scientific research, a device which gives measurements about some natural phenomenon which the scientist wishes to investigate.  Warner (1990) argues that the term 'scientific instrument' does not deserve the extensive use which has been made of it, at least by historians.  She traces the trajectory of terms from the mid-seventeenth century, when a distinct class of 'philosophical' instruments began to be marked off from musical, medical and mathematical apparatus.  I am not concerned here, however, with historical exactitude, but with the use of the term to invoke the qualities which are generally understood to be invested in an adequate instrument: validity and reliability in representation of an underlying natural phenomenon.

The role of scientific instruments in extending the senses of the scientist, to make new phenomena available for comment, is documented by Schaffer (1989), in his discussion of Newton's prisms.  Schaffer analyses the work which goes into making the prisms 'transparent' as instruments (Schaffer, 1989, p. 70), in the sense that they come to demonstrate a phenomenon truly existing in nature, and the prisms themselves become 'untroubled objects' (Schaffer, 1989, p. 99).

This concept has much resonance with the process described by Laour and Woolgar (1986) as 'black boxing'. This process they see as kept in the laboratory, in enabling pieces of apparatus to produce 'immutable mobiles': the inscriptions which circulate within and outside the laboratory as exemplars of underlying phenomena. Workers in the sociology of science (Latour & Woolgar, 1986; Gooding *et al.*, 1989) have used Bachelard's notion of the scientific instrument as reified or embodied theory, to draw out the sense in which the inner working of the instrument can come to seem beyond question in its everyday operation. Baird (1993) draws further on this to express an idea that the received status of the instrument as beyond question can itself lend legitimacy to the claims of science:

> Instrumentation has become one important standard for objectivity, and in so doing it has become one important channel for the expression and development of scientific knowledge (p. 288).

Baird (1993), Baird and Faust (1990) and Blume (1992) suggest that the role played by instruments in science has been neglected, in comparison to the extensive considerations of theory as representing knowledge. Baird (1993) argues for the specific inclusion of scientific instruments in the philosophy of science:

> ... when I say that both instruments and theory are final goods of science, I mean that both tell us what the world is like. Scientific instruments are elements of scientific knowledge.

Baird (1993) counters the view that scientific revolutions are always theoretical in nature, positing a revolution in analytical chemistry, and more generally, with the advent of widespread instrumentation. He does concede, however, that "the introduction of instruments in analytical chemistry altered the form which analytical theory could take. While, clearly, the instruments did not alter the form of theory itself, they did provide a new kind of outlet for analytical knowledge - instrumentation" (Baird, 1993, p. 285) We therefore have a dual picture of the scientific instrument, which involves it standing for a body of accepted theory, but also making possible the development of theory in certain directions.

Blume (1992) suggests that new attention is indeed being paid to the role of scientific instruments, both by those who study science and by scientists themselves:

> Experimental scientists are well aware of the definitive significance for their work of instrumentation, and the ways in which it is used. The new interest of

historians and sociologists of science in studying the material culture finds constant resonance in natural scientists' own reflections and musings (p.88).

The above give arguments for paying attention to scientific instruments. But already we have something of a paradox: Blume suggests that the instruments are a source of constant reflection for scientists, but Schaffer (1989) seems to suggest that the instruments become transparent. This suggests that possibly instruments are not the fixed and inflexible entities which they might appear to be. Instruments may have, instead, an important role to play in scientific narrative (both of scientists and of those who study science), and twists in the plot for particular purposes may be achieved by their appearance and disappearance, the ways in which they recede into the background or advance into the foreground. My thesis is that IT as a scientific instrument is involved in a complex co-construction of self, instrument and genetic object for the scientist, and further that this co-construction is strategically varied as the prevailing narrative requires. This observation will form a theme for the ethnographic part of this chapter. The next section prepares the ground for this analysis by looking in more detail at some of the roles which have been imputed to laboratory technology by sociologists and historians of science. These roles are concerned with: the construction of expertise; the organisation of research; experimentation; discovery; and research directions.

*What Role is Played in the Construction of Expertise?*

The roles which scientific instruments may play in laboratory life and labour are introduced by Blume (1992), in his analysis of the nostalgia stories of experienced scientists, for the old days when less sophisticated instruments were available, and scientists had to be able to build or mend them:

> ... experimentation, doing things, building things, fiddling, would have to be constitutive of the period of their careers which elderly successful scientists looking back see as formative, having made them what they are (p.90).

This suggests that instruments, or interaction with them, may play an important part in some stores of what makes laboratory work skilled. The changes which may occur in involvement with instruments throughout a scientific career are depicted in the following passage:

> Learning to do things with instruments, to manipulate them, to judge the significance of the data they yield, to deploy them in experiment ... these things

are of the essence of the scientific apprenticeship. The mature scientist, advanced in his career, spends his time doing very different things ... perhaps for many the closest they get is vicarious experimentation. They design experiments, interpret results, theorise, but with rare exceptions do not themselves engage in 'hands in' experimental practice (p. 90).

This excerpt suggests that skilled interaction with instruments is an important part of the individual scientist's career. Use of instruments may also change through the history of a discipline. Baird (1993) notes a complaint of an analytical chemist, Liebhafsky, that the coming of instrumentation in the discipline led to a general deskilling of the work. This was a deskilling in contrast to the 'old ways', in which the achievement of results was dependent on experience and proficiency in the use of instruments and techniques. Deskilling, and subsequent loss of status, is brought into focus here, rather than increased efficiency or reliability of achieving results.

The role played by 'tinkering' with scientific instruments is stressed by Mukerji (1992), who suggests that these activities lead to even standardised instruments possessing a 'laboratory signature'. Practical experience may come to seem indistinguishable from the machine itself, use of the instrument relying on the operation of practice, and vice versa:

> ... any instrument merges in practice with procedures and techniques, both practical and theoretical (Bud & Cozzens, 1992, p. xii).

These stories suggest that even for an accepted and seemingly standardised instrument or technique, there are narrative circumstances in which the skill required to operate it comes to the fore. Jordan and Lynch (1992) show for the plasmid preparation that closure, stabilisation or black boxing is a contingent and reversible process - the technique becomes a standardised yet local achievement. There is therefore some suggestion that while use of an instrument is productive for science, mere usage is not enough for certain narrative purposes: for these, one has to have been inside the machine and seen what it does. In these stories, mere use of the machine comes to be seen as unskilled and routine.

## What Role is Played in the Organisation of Science?

A further issue which has been of note to historians and sociologists of science is the changing sites of production and use of scientific instruments. Warner (1990) describes, along with the advent of recognised scientific instruments, the growth in recognised forms of scientific instrument makers.

Blume suggests that a process of commodification of science is occurring, as large and expensive instruments come to seem indispensable to the doing of science. He suggests that this may be part of a consumer culture emerging in science, in which the properties of the instruments themselves come to seem increasingly irrelevant:

> The significance of acquiring the most advanced and powerful instrumentation is to be understood in relation to the need to enhance status within the 'organisational field' and thereby to maintain one's competitive advantage (p. 98).

This commodification is also linked to a growing use of standardised instruments, as Blume argues:

> ... the pressures under which research laboratories today operate, with emphasis on efficiency, selling services, and so on, make increasing recourse to standardised equipment a wise strategy (p. 97).

Fujimura (1987) suggests that 'standardised packages' of tools and techniques may take problems more do-able, by extending the availability of the resources to deal with a phenomenon to a wider range of laboratories.

These observations suggest a growing pressure for the separation of producer and consumer roles in the development and use of scientific instruments. The industrialisation of scientific instrument production has implications for the ability of the scientist and phenomenon. There is not, however, a complete separation between instrument makers and scientists:

> Scientists clearly do get involved in the development of instruments, in particular because of their ability to merge scientific and technical aims in the process of scientific work. Instrument makers, likewise, do interact with the laboratory as they develop and define new products (Bud & Cozzens, 1992, p. xiii).

Where there are no obvious rewards from the scientific system, it may seem appropriate to relegate the development of instruments to an industrial sphere. The organisation of science, and the allocation of roles of instrument developer and instrument user therefore depends and draws on a number of conflicting narratives: those of scientific expertise; efficiency and economics; professional boundaries; and reward structures. Again, the role played by instruments is not fixed, but is flexible according to the demands of the context.

*What Role is Played in Discovery Stories?*

The previous sections have dealt with situations in which the presence of instruments is foregrounded, and it is the nature of the instrument which is in question. There are circumstances, however, in which the instrument takes a background, passive role against a foreground of active scientist and scientific object.

Latour (1992) has it that the scientific paper is free to distribute the parts in its narratives between humans and non-humans:

> This freedom in selecting actors and redistributing properties among them is crucial to understanding scientific practice, and, to my knowledge, no other discipline possesses that freedom (p.131).

In scientific papers, the instrument may play a very minor role, a mere facilitator, because centre stage is given to the phenomenon. The instrument is present merely to give a voice to an underlying scientific object.

The scientific instrument in typical discovery stories of the heroic scientist plays an absent, or relegated, role. When it comes to the telling of discovery stories, centre stage is given to human endeavour, to a moment of inspiration in a human mind. The Nobel Prize is presented to the scientist who 'makes' the discovery, rather than the instrument which makes the discovery possible.

*What Role is Played in Experiment?*

To focus in further on scientific practice, the site of use of a scientific instrument is often understood to be the experiment. Blume (1992) suggests that the instrument is involved as one actor in a scene occupied also by practice and theory. He considers that the scientist is attempting to bring into alignment these three different facets of science:

> In experimenting, in trying to generate what colleagues will regard as plausible knowledge claims (Pickering speaks simply of 'facts'), the scientist is seeking coherence between his material practice (what he does: setting up the apparatus, running it ...), his instrumental model (his understanding of how the apparatus works: the understanding that goes into the design of the experiment); and his phenomenal model (his understanding of the part of the world under investigation: the relevant theory in the sense the word is generally used, shared with his professional community) (p. 92).

Latour (1992) puts it more succinctly:

> What is an experiment? It is an action performed by the scientist so that the nonhuman will be made to appear on its own (p. 141).

The role played by theory in experiment is disputed by Bud and Cozzens (1992), who consider that the instrument provides the scientist with the freedom to explore without having formulated a specific theoretical position:

> Instruments provide for exploration and play in the experimental sciences. They allow scientists to explore tentatively at the edges of what is known, without the constraints of deductive theorising (p, xii).

Focusing on the practice of experiment, Collins (1985) observes that the point at which the instrument is deemed to be properly working is itself a subject for negotiation. The position given to the scientific instrument in experiment is therefore open to consideration as a rhetorical device, as much as the role it plays in scientific careers:

> Recovering the role of instruments in experiment represents an important advance in the understanding of how scientists achieve certainty (Gooding *et al.,* 1989, p. 5).

Again in experiment, as for expertise, organisation and discovery, we find that instruments play multiple and flexible narrative roles.

## *What Role is Played in Scientific Research Directions?*

A final consideration regarding the many characters of scientific instruments is the roles which they may be attributed in the determination of the birth of disciplines and new research directions. The invention of a new instrument, or the introduction of an instrument into a new field, can play a part in the creation of new phenomena for a field to study and in providing for new directions of research.

Gokalp (1990) suggests that there are three main ways in which new instruments are introduced into the 'instrumentation space' of a discipline: borrowing from other fields; evolution of an existing technique; adoption of a totally new technique. It is suggested that each of these has different implications for changes in organisation and knowledge within the discipline. In the case which is described in detail, it is suggested that new instruments had a unifying effect on a 'borderland' area of scientific practice:

> The point I want to stress is that the material practice of science (establishing the scope and nature of a series of experiments, choosing or designing the instrumentation to be used, making the observations) and the kind of negotiations which experimentation involves (with professional peers, laboratory heads, funding bodies of various kinds) are inter-dependent (Blume, 1992, p. 93).

The ways of incorporating a new instrument into the laboratory range from "creative tinkering to perfunctory consumption", according to Bud and Cozzens (1992, p. 85). The tools of a discipline, may, however, change through time:

> For they may have political careers, intellectual careers, moral careers and/or technical careers, which may be all bound up together (Clarke & Fujimura, 1992, p. 16).

Keating *et al.* (1992) show the importance of attending to the disciplinary level as well as the individual laboratory in considering a scientific instrument. They show the effects which disciplines can have on tools as well as the effects which tools can have on disciplines, in their consideration of the affinity/avidity debate in immunology. This contrasts with the deterministic stance of Gokalp (1990), who has it that particular kinds of instrumental innovation bring with them different effects on scientific disciplines. Keating *et al.* 1992) brings out the point that 'progress' is a question of articulation between the nature of the discipline and the nature of its tools.


## Problems for a Study of IT as a Scientific Instrument

The studies of scientific instruments described above have shown that they are not neutral tools, the silent servants of an inevitable trajectory of scientific progress. Rather, they are active agents which can also be used strategically in the construction of laboratory work, skill and expertise, discovery and disciplinary development. The study of scientific instruments, as has been shown above, provides opportunities for discussing many fundamental issues of science. This suggests that, rather than needing to make a case for IT in genetics as being something new, exciting and altogether different, analytic purchase may be afforded by considering the role which it plays as a scientific instrument. I will be particularly concerned, in the latter parts of this paper, to demonstrate the co-

constructions of scientist, technology and genetic object, and to suggest how these change in different circumstances. I show that the use of IT is strategic, facultative and motivated, both in the sense of everyday laboratory work and in the narrative purposes which it serves.

The following excerpts are drawn from a series of interviews conducted during a phase of ethnographic observation, at a laboratory in central London conducting research connected with human genome mapping. The interviewees included doctoral students and postdoctoral researchers, who were asked biographical questions about their career trajectories, and the ways in which they had come to use IT in their work.

## Self, Technology and Object

The stories which were told in the interviews about the technology, especially about making practical use of IT, were frequently characterised by juxtapositions of self-descriptions with descriptions of the technology. The PhD student in the following excerpt characterises herself and the technology, in a story of what the undoubted capabilities of the technology would have been if only she, herself, had not been afraid to use them:

> So I was really scared of databases and you know in my third year when I started generating all the data I should have been inputting the data into the database, and it's only like towards the end of the third year I realised what a fool I'd been, because I wouldn't touch the computer. I was just so scared, I thought I'm going to press something and everything's going to be scrapped, and it's going to be everybody else's data. You know, if I had started, I mean what I'd been doing was I'd been generating the results and I'd be writing it down. If I had started putting it into the computer, the computer would have been giving me feedback of where I was going wrong, which just looking at results doesn't give, so in a sense I was making myself more work, because towards the end I had to repeat a lot of the work (interview 1, lines 140-162).

In other narratives, the technology was found to be a fault for failures in use, requiring a characterisation of a competent self to operate it. This excerpt from a postdoctoral researcher illustrates the point, with a characterisation of a competent self as one experienced with the technology:

> Just because I was doing, you know, I've done it more than anyone else I think, I've done a lot of homology searching, and primer design and stuff like that. You know I kind of, I don't know, I pick it up quite easily I think as well. But I don't

think the programmes in the [ ] are not user friendly at all I would say (interview 9, lines 2412-2420).

In these excerpts, we therefore have the beginning of a process in which the scientific self is defined in relation to the technology which is used in the laboratory. But this leaves in question the nature of the object which is 'seen' through use of IT. Interpreting results was also portrayed in some circumstances as straightforward, in a story in which the computer 'tells' the scientist something:

> If I had started putting it into the computer, the computer would have been giving me feedback of where I was going wrong, which just looking at results doesn't give (interview 1, lines 155-160).

In other situations, however, the reading of results from the computer is portrayed as non-straightforward, as requiring skill and experience to determine what the outcome is:

> And homology searching, when you get the results you get Poisson probabilities and everything, and there's no real explanation, there's a score and there's no real explanation of what the score means or where they get the score from, what the probability, I've kind of worked it out just by kind of thinking myself, just from kind of general principles that I know, which are the significant match ups and which aren't (interview 9, lines 2440-2451).

In the stories which are told about past discoveries, of gene characterisations and mappings, the role of IT becomes suddenly quiet. We are given a picture of a scientist physically involved with the work - 'pulling out' genes and clones, 'looking' at candidate genes:

> I'm actually screening cDNA libraries now trying to pull out the full spliced gene, the full coding region (interview 4, lines 832-835).

> ... from then on basically doing some work on genes within the region and looking at various candidate genes to see whether they were the ( ) gene or not (interview 6, lines 1428-1432).

This presents a picture of the use of IT as an occupation which involves the telling of stories to rationalise the identity of the scientist, the instrument and the object. In telling their stories, the geneticists draw on a range of available characterisations. Where the instrument is in focus, the scientist may be characterised as adept and the machine difficult, resulting in a skilled scientist. By contrast, the telling of discovery stories may require an active scientist and a silent technology, such that the object appears as self-evident.

## IT and Learning

For analytic purposes, I have focused in this paper on IT as a scientific instrument. There are also situations in the laboratory in which the characterisation of IT as just another scientific instrument arises. These were frequently concerned in interviews with the questions about how use of IT was learned.

None of those questioned had any formal training in computing, beyond a few who had experienced introductory programming or statistical courses as undergraduates. Manuals for using various packages did exist in the laboratory, but were hard to find when needed, and rarely sought. Rather, emphasis was placed on learning to use packages by being shown personally by someone who already used them. Where there were problems, interviewees often said that they would ask someone who was around, rather than use the manual or one of the official sources such as electronic mail or telephone help lines. This has much in common with the laboratory wisdom that even where a full protocol is available for a new technique, it is better to be shown how to do it personally by someone who is already adept:

> I generally try to find someone who's done it before because I think that's by far and away the best way of learning it, because even if you go to a paper and the technique is there in point form, one to ten, there's quite often subtle little bits which they don't put in which make all the difference, and if you find someone who does it hands on you pick up these subtle little bits rather than just reading it (interview 11, lines 2918-2929).

In their learning practices, the geneticists interviewed treated the use of IT as analogous with the protocols which were learnt by demonstration. The description of learning often entails characterising certain individuals as naturally skilled or interested in the use of computers, and therefore as people to be learnt from:

> That's it, none of us get a course, you just hope that you can rely on somebody who's been on one or has done it before, or who has an interest naturally in computers (interview 4, lines 1071-1075).

> Well, from people here basically, who learned by trial and error generally. You know, when we started, there were other people here at the time who were relatively proficient in computer usage and one of them in particular spent more

time on the computer than at the bench and just loved computing, so that was quite good, in all sorts of way, he did lots of favours for us and we did learn quite a lot from him that way (interview 6, lines 1528-1540).

Describing the process of learning to use IT therefore involves the positioning of oneself and others with respect to the technology, and the positioning of the technology with respect to other laboratory instruments.

*IT and Time*

Interviewees were asked when they did the majority of their computing: was it at particular times of the day, or on particular days, or was it at particular stages of the project? The picture of sequence which emerged was one in which the use of IT took a strategic part in projects: yes, it was an intrinsic part of the work, but it was indicated at particular stages and for particular purposes. For example, in this excerpt, the use of a particular program could provide another piece of evidence to align with others in the characterisation of a found mutation as the mutation which causes a particular disease:

> I mean another thing I wanted to do recently was to get a nice 3D kind of or a 2D cartoon of a protein to look at folding, because we're looking at mutations you see, and it would be interesting for me to know if we find a mutation, what effect it might have on the folding you know, so I can just look at it, will it really, will it really disrupt it if I look at it now, so it's obvious it's a horrible shape compared to normal (interview 9, lines 2527-2538).

Another excerpt also illustrates this point about strategic use:

> Usually when you do some sequencing or you're finding out about a project or you find something interesting like we found out that one of our sequences had a homology to myosin, the next thing that you  have to do is try and get references, as many references as possible concerning myosin, its function, where it's found and things like that (interview 4, lines 1004-1014).

The use of IT had also to fit into the routines of other parts of laboratory work, as did these interviews. Time was scheduled such that other tasks were fitted into the demands of PCR machines and electrophoretic gels. These took precedence. Time on the computer was also generally agreed to be different to time spent doing laboratory work: there was a need for quietness and seclusion, such that computer work was conducted late at night, or at home, or at the weekends:

> The offices aren't very good, they're a bit claustrophobic, people around, it's a bit, you know, a little bit incestuous, people looking over your shoulder all the time, you don't really feel comfortable, you just want to get on with it, you don't want to be bothered basically, and it's better when it's quieter basically (interview 6, lines 1681-1689).

This portrayal of IT use as something which just fits in with other work, which can be saved for quieter times, and which is only indicated at certain stages of a project, leads to a picture of IT as a strategic technology in laboratory work. The strategic uses of IT are two-fold: in the sense that it is a technology used at certain times, rather than a constant feature of the work; and in the deeper sense that it is used as a strategic resource in describing research processes and outcomes.

## Conclusion: Strategy and Motivation

Few of the interviewees portrayed themselves as the disciplined users envisaged by the designers of the technology (Hine, 1995). By contrast, they portrayed their use of IT as strategic. It was a motivated usage, portrayed as being demanded at certain stages of the project in the development of a new object, but rarely carried out for its own sake. The usage of IT is facultative, in that in the discovery stories it is portrayed as non-essential, just another piece of support for the current theory. In short, it is strategic use of a piece of technology as part of a process of fact construction. The upshot is a characterised or mapped gene.

I took as my frame for this analysis of IT as a scientific instrument the frame offered by Clarke and Fujimura (1992) of co-construction. I concentrated on self, technology and object, while Clarke and Fujimura concerned themselves with tools, jobs and rightness. Clarke and Fujimura considered there to be three elements to the co-construction of jobs, tools and rightness: constructing do-able problems; crafting and tinkering; and standardisation, stabilisation and deployment of results. Through these processes, they suggest that scientific instruments acquire symbolic status:

> That is, tools are not neutral objects but through their use in practice-in interactive situations-become meaning-laden entities to all those familiar with them for any reason (p. 16).

In considering the elements of co-construction of self, technology and objects in the case of IT in the laboratory, I have shown that an array of available resources, including career narratives for selves, technologies and objects, are drawn upon. The technology of the scientific instrument is foregrounded and backgrounded at strategic points in these narratives, such that scientific heroism and creativity, objectivity and a transparent view of nature, and a definite genetic object are able to appear. What might seem paradoxical from a survey of the sociological and historical literature on scientific instruments, that instruments could be represented as requiring great skill to use and yet still give unquestionable access to objective truth, is dealt with in the laboratory on a daily basis.

## References

Baird, D. (1993) Analytical chemistry and the 'big' scientific instrumentation revolution. *Annals of Science*, **50**, 267-290.

Baird, D. & Faust, T. (1990) Scientific instruments, scientific progress and the Cyclotron. *British Journal of the Philosophy of Science*, **41**, 147-175.

Blume, S. (1992) Whatever happened to the string and sealing wax? In Bud, R. & Cozzens, S. (eds) Invisible Connections: Instruments, Institutions and ScienceSPIE Optical Engineering Press, Bellingham, Washington, 87-101.

Bud, R. & Cozzens, S. (eds) (1992) *Invisible Connections: Instruments,Institutions and Science*. SPIE Optical Engineering Press, Bellingham, Washington.

Clarke, A.E. & Fujimura, J.H. (eds) (1992) *The Right Tools for the Job: At Work in Twentieth-century Life Sciences*. Princeton University, Press, Princeton.

Collins, H. (1985) *Changing Order: Replication and Induction in Scientific Practice*. Sage, Beverley Hills, California.

Fujimura, J. (1987) Constructing do-able problems in cancer research: articulating alignment. *Social Studies of Science*, **17**, 257-293.

Gokalp, I. (1990) Turbulent reactions: impact of new instrumentation on a borderland scientific domain. *Science, Technology and Human Values*, **15**, 284-304.

Gooding, D, Pinch, T & Schaffer, S. (eds) (1989) *The Uses of Experiment: Studies in the Natural Sciences*. Cambridge University Press, Cambridge.

Hine, C.M. (1995) Ethnography and relevance: empowering the virtual end user? CRICT Discussion Paper.

Jordan, K. & Lynch, M. (1992) The sociology of a genetic engineering technique: ritual and rationality in the performance of the 'plasmid prep'. In Clarke, A.E. & Fujimura, J. (eds) *The Right Tools for the Job: At Work in Twentieth-century Life Sciences*. Princeton University Press, Princeton, 77-114.

Keating, P., Cambrosio, A. & Mackenzie, M. (1992) The tools of the discipline: standards, models and measures in the affinity/avidity controversy in immunology. In Clarke, A.E. & Fujimura, J. (eds) *The Right Tools for the Job: At Work in Twentieth-century Life Sciences*. Princeton University Press, Princeton, 312-354.

Latour, B. (1992) Pasteur on lactic acid yeast: a partial semiotic analysis. *Configurations*, **1**, 129-145.

Latour, B. & Woolgar, S, (1986) *Laboratory Life: The Construction of Scientific Facts*, 2nd edn. Princeton University Press, Princeton.

Mukerji, C. (1992) Scientific techniques and learning: laboratory signatures and the practice of oceanography. In Bud, R. & Cozzens, S. (eds) *Invisible Connections: Instruments, Institutions and Science.* SPIE Optical Engineering Press, Bellingham, Washington, 102-129.

Schaffer, S. (1989) Glass works: Newton's prisms and the uses of experiment. In Gooding, D., Pinch, T. & Schaffer, S. (eds) *The Uses of Experiment: Studies in the Natural Sciences.* Cambridge University Press, Cambridge, 67-104.

Warner, D.J. (1990) What is a scientific instrument, when did it become one, and why? *British Journal of the History of Science*, **23**, 83-93.

# 5 Exploring Organisational Issues in British Genomic Research

PETER GLASNER, HARRY ROTHMAN & DAVID TRAVIS

ABSTRACT     *Genome mapping is not a single funded enterprise but consists of several national and international programmes conducted in numerous institutions and funded from a variety of sources. While this pluralistic structure allows more flexibility and choice of routes early in the research process, it also creates considerable problems of coordination and collaboration for the various participants. This is further complicated by national, commercial and individual rivalries. While there has been some sociological research on the ways in which governments balance the demands for scientific growth and development with the pressures for accountability and economic productivity, genomic research illustrates the need to integrate these into a wider framework. This is particularly pertinent given its significant social implications for health and medicine, and the very public debate over patenting and intellectual property rights. The key question to be addressed in this chapter is whether any lessons for future policy can be drawn from the different modes of management and organisation currently operating in the UK Focusing on the Medical Research Council's Human Genome Mapping Project, it investigates the processes of prioritisation of objectives, the linkages between individuals and organisations, the problems of coordination and communication, and the changing bases for funding.*

## Introduction

The transnational nature of contemporary scientific research in molecular biology is well illustrated by the ambitious programme designed to produce complete genetic and physical maps of the human genome (Office of Technology Assessment, 1988; Bishop & Waldholz, 1990; Davis, 1990). The UK programme is regarded as one of the major contributors to genomic research, and has a long history of research in molecular biology centred on key institutions (Judson, 1979; Bud, 1994). British genomic research has succeeded in attracting funding from both government sources and private charities. The Medical Research Council (MRC) is responsible for the UK Human Genome Mapping Programme (UK HGMP), including the Resource Centre and the Directed Programme of funding, and, more recently, the programme on Genetic Approaches to Human Health. The Biotechnology and Biological Sciences Research Council (BBSRC) funds work on farm animals and crop genotypes. The two major charities, the Wellcome Trust and the Imperial Cancer Research Fund, support independent research laboratories like the Sanger Centre, the Human Genome Organisation (HUGO, Europe), libraries and data banks.

The UK effort must however be seen as part of a European commitment to developing this area, even more so following the European Commission's December 1994 agreement on a substantial budget as part of the Fourth RTD Framework Programme *(Genome Digest,* January 1995, p. 11). The management and organisation of genomic research in Europe does not follow a single pattern, and takes several forms. At one level, the European Commission in Brussels, and the Human Genome Organisation (HUGO, Europe) with its headquarters in London, provide coordinating and strategic roles, along with the European Molecular Biology Organisation (EMBO) and UNESCO (McLaren, 1992). At another level, various UK laboratories form integral parts of European-funded networks such as BRIDGE (Biotechnology Research for Innovation, Development and Growth) in Europe (Magnien *et al.,* 1992), and BAP (Biotechnology Action Programme) (Vassarotti & Goffeau, 1992). A European consortium of yeast artificial chromosome (YAC) screening centres, including the UK HGMP Resource Centre, was established under the EC Biomed 1 Programme in 1994 (Gibson, 1995). These various national and international programmes pose interesting problems both for participating individuals and organisations, and their governments.

The problems have been brought into sharp focus in the UK following the 1993 White Paper on a future policy for science and technology (HMSO, 1993). This focused on the need to improve innovation and wealth creation in the context of user needs. Webster (1991) has noted the paucity of research on the ways in which governments balance the demands for scientific growth and development with the pressures for accountability and economic productivity, although some have been completed in the field of strategic management (e.g. Macharzina & Staehle, 1986). This seems particularly to be the case in biotechnology, where research has focused instead on the way it is regulated (Bennett *et al.,* 1986), the construction of 'do-able' research (Fujimara, 1987), the process of technology transfer (Webster, 1990) and commercialisation (Yoxen, 1983). Genomic research, with its wider social implications for health and medicine (Kevles & Hood, 1992), and the very public debate over patenting and intellectual property rights (Anderson, 1991) illustrates the need to integrate these earlier studies into wider issues. This paper will attempt to develop a framework for this process of integration by focusing on the Resource Centre established by the MRC as part of the UK HGMP. In order to facilitate this, four key issues will be discussed:

- the process of prioritising scientific objectives;
- the networks between individuals and organisations;
- the problems of coordination and communication;
- the changing bases for funding.

Data has been drawn from interviews with key participants in the operation of the Resource Centre, various official surveys and reports, and a wide range of primary and secondary sources.

## Prioritising Objectives

It was perhaps inevitable that senior British scientists would have been pressing government and the research councils for earmarked funding for genomic research from the late 1980s, given the strong tradition of work in molecular biology in the UK. This was especially true in the competitive context of the US Office of Technology Assessment's report (OTA, 1988) which endorsed a programme costing up to three billion dollars lasting well into the next century. The establishment of HUGO at the Cold Spring Harbour meeting in 1988 to promote international coordination of human genome research also owed much to the participation of British scientists (Bodmer, 1990). In the event, an additional, 'ring-fenced', 3-year budget of £11 million was made available to the MRC, at a

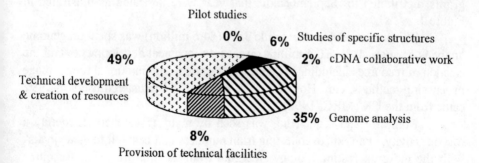

**Figure 1.** Pie Chart distribution grants by UK HGMP up to September 1992.

time in 1989 when spending on the science base in the UK was settled in a 'steady state' (Ziman, 1987). This was increased by a further £4.5 million in 1992, consolidated into the Grant-in-Aid and allocated specifically for genome research (OST, 1994). (For more detail, see the chapter by Balmer in this book.)

A proportion of the funds went to establish the HGMP Resource Centre at the Clinical Research Centre of the Northwick Park Hospital in Harrow. This was designed as a national facility providing services and reagents to the entire UK scientific community. It is the national repository and site for systematic programmes of data generation, and a reference and distribution centre for human and mouse mapping resources. It also provides computing facilities and access to international databases. Services to its over 1000, mainly academic, users are free in return for data deposition (OST, 1994). An analysis of the projects linked in the Resource Centre network include those dealing with human disease such as Alzheimer's, motor neurone, schizophrenia and obesity; those dealing with non-human genomes including mouse, pig, nematode, drosophila and yeast; and those developing and improving methods and techniques including computational systems, YAC libraries, cell banks and *in-situ* hybridisation.

Interviews (March 1993, January 1994) with the staff at the Resource Centre suggest that the first year of operation was largely a wasted opportunity, and it was only with the arrival of its first manager, Tony Vickers, that a more focused approach was developed. Vickers believed that a pragmatic, 'value-for-money' philosophy was required. Rather than spend time playing with different models of organisational structure, and allocating funds to existing 'barons', it was necessary for the centre to develop deliverable services linked to performance indicators. The money was there to be spent, but so was the need to set the MRC HGMP apart from the others. The 1992 manager's report to the MRC reveals that grants distributed to September of that year were allocated as illustrated in Figure 1.

This makes it clear that while 35% (£4.6 million) was spent on genome analysis as such, 49% (£6.4 million) went into technical developments and the creation of resources including sequencing, libraries, computational tools, image processing methods, etc. However, 84% of the 1364 registered users in 1992 came from the UK (MRC, 1992).

Mapping and sequencing was seen by many researchers as merely a routine activity, more akin to collecting train numbers and best left to 'gene jocks', with the more interesting biology emerging from its spin-offs. The Resource Centre has attempted to facilitate the development of more interesting research by providing broad support for the biological research community, and attracting industrial partners into its network. In this latter area, significant success has so far proved elusive, with only a handful of paying users attracted from industry (OST, 1994).

## Networks

Hilgartner (1994, pp. 306 *et seq.*) has suggested, in the context of the US, that the HGMP differs from other biological research in that it is conducted by mainly small groups of scientists, contributing to a clearly defined long-term goal. This focusing of attention has implications not only because biologists "lack an established set of off-the-shelf organisational mechanisms or cultural resources to draw on", but because of the complexity engendered by the international distribution of laboratory work. He goes on to note:

> As is typical of the development of a technological system, the task of constructing the genome project involves an inextricable mix of problems with technical, economic, organisational and political dimensions.

Some solutions to these problems, as we have suggested, have been addressed in the UK through the development of the HGMP Resource Centre. In this respect, it could provide a concrete example of 'heterogeneous engineering' (Law, 1987) - an attempt to link together networks of people, laboratories, funding, policies, databases, materials, etc. Vinck *et al.* (1993) developing a similar approach in relation to AIDS, propose the concept of a scientific cooperation network which, in addition to being heterogeneous, is flexible and progressive.

In the early stages of the development of the Resource Centre, funding for universities was based on a distributed programme of research and administered by the Directed Programme Committee, including representatives of what came to be called the CLEO group -researchers at the university of Cambridge, London, Edinburgh and Oxford. There was some feeling (in interviews ) that most of the money ended up with the CLEO group. Interestingly, members of this group also appeared to play similar roles in some of the major funding charities (Balmer, 1993). This was interpreted more as an example of the existing structures of power and control within the British scientific establishment than anything reflecting a wider range of networks. It did however have the consequence that some work was funded which may not have achieved a high alpha rating, based on its scientific novelty value, in open competition with biologists not concerned with the programme, and this added to the feelings of resentment.

The Resource Centre was the focus for a diverse range of different networks in addition to CLEO, whose importance waned as the bureaucratic structure of the organisation of the UK HGMP was slowly simplified. Research grants were distributed for the provision of technical facilities such as imaging equipment, lasers, etc. and for technical developments and resources including libraries, computational tools, image processing, etc. as well as the range of mapping and sequencing activity. Training programmes were developed for facilitating access to the databases both here and abroad. Workshops and 'users meetings' were used to bring members of the UK genome community together on a regular basis. Materials, such as YACs, were distributed and received, and researchers in difficulties invited to resolve them by visiting the centre in person. All of these activities appear to contribute to making the HGMP Resource Centre the nodal point of a rich and variegated cooperative and heterogeneous network (MRC, 1991, 1992).

Discussions with staff at the Resource Centre also illustrate the extent to which technical requirements have helped to structure the development of the science. This has been especially true at the level of data collection and storage. Ritter (1994, p.10) has noted that:

> Today, genome researchers need to access dozens of major resources and hundreds of computational tools to work with information on bimolecular structures and sequences, genetic and genomic maps, phenotypes, biological material and reagents, individual experiments, bibliography, community contact data, etc.

Following Star and Ruhleder (1994), there is evidence of gaps between designers of the systems and the system users, the extent to which knowledge of the systems is completely shared by the users themselves, and the gap between the routines and the rapidly growing infrastructure (and see chapter by Hine in this book). The provision of computing service is, as one respondent to the User Survey noted, "absolutely essential to small groups like ourselves with limited resources" (Bates, 1992). The computing manager's 1992 report states clearly that the "network, as the medium of information dissemination, is the computer" (MRC, 1992, p.11), and indicates that user support may need to grow as much as 30% per annum.

While some respondents felt that the service functioned very efficiently, this was not a uniformly held view ("Work on the computer takes hours..."), and some software difficulties were manifest. Thus, one user felt that the database was "not very user friendly", and several wanted what another summarised as a "simple, easy to follow, guide to data bank screening, file management, etc. (for the beginner)". However, there is evidence to suggest that the Resource Centre may already act in what Star and Ruhleder describe as an example of those systems developed for collaborative scientific work involving geographically dispersed researchers, i.e. a 'collaboratory'. Certainly, many of the difficulties mentioned are likely to be exacerbated by the use made of the centre by many researchers for whom mapping the human genome is by no means their primary concern. As Ritter (1995, p. 12) suggests, in discussing the plans for an integrated genomic database:

> What makes the genome information management problem so challenging is not only the sheer volume of generated data and derived information, but primarily the high diversity, complexity, and dynamics of the information models we have to deal with.

## Coordination and Communication

The role played by the Resource Centre encourages the continuation of the kind of the small group research identified by Hilgartner, and established the possibility of an alternative, longer term infrastructure, in no small part based upon the use of computing technology. According to Tony Vickers, the outgoing centre manager (interview, March 1993), the Centre set out to encourage a culture of cooperation and collectivism based upon the principle of free exchange of information, This had the consequence of enabling smaller research groups to participate on a more 'level playing field' in the distribution of research funds once the centre had become established. It also had the latent function of enroling peripheral researchers whose primary motivation was often focused on the health-related aspects of the research rather than the HGMP.

Since many researchers were, indeed, more interested in health-related research, Vickers was concerned that one of the key measures of communication (and of course a key index of the programme's success) - publication in journals devoted to genomic research - was missing. Conventional bibliometric techniques were not sufficiently developed to scan the wide range of possible outlets and citation counts appeared to seriously under-represent the quality and quantity of genomic research achievement (Balmer & Martin, 1991). This approach underplays the significance of the research-related information either generated by the Resource Centre or following through its networks. In particular, it ignores the physical research products such as experimental materials, innovative instruments, software and data sets, as well as the actual research techniques ('craft knowledge') which were being developed both centrally, and in the distributed, and often geographically very separate, research teams. It takes no account of the manuals, individual communications, laboratory visits, courses and workshops, which help to induct neophytes into the Resource Centre network, or the extent to which different forms of knowledge are required, and shared, in the day-to-day use of genome mapping technology (Cambrosio & Keating, 1988). For, as McCain (1991) notes, tacit knowledge may play a more significant role in the biological sciences than it does elsewhere.

Bibliometric evaluation also overlooks another significant aspect of the MRC programme. The user/grantee contracts to make the results of research freely available on the Centre database. Access to Resource Centre data and materials, as well as being a condition of grants awarded under the directed programme, as noted earlier, is free but based on reciprocity. This has the effect of enshrining the ethos of sharing, outlined by Merton (1973) in his classic discussion of the normative structure of science, within a political and technical framework. Hilgartner (1994, p. 312), in analysing a similar role for sequence-tagged sites in the US HGMP, suggests that
social control can be seen as directly, and materially, built into the 'very fabric of scientific production'.

Measuring the success of the Resource Centre has been possible through the mail survey of users already mentioned (Bates, 1992). This provided information about the extent to which the range of available resources has been taken up by respondents, and comments about their levels of satisfaction. It supplemented the existing utilisation records collected on a day-to-day basis by centre staff. In theory, the centre has also been in a position to evaluate both the quality, and the quantity, of the data requested and submitted, as a further tool for enhancing control, and facilitating its accountability to the outside world. It could, in principle, develop input/output measures for all registered users and use these to improve performance indicators.

Finally, a degree of cooperation for mutual advantage has been established in loose knit associations or consortia which are linking together to produce a publicly available human gene map early in the next millennium (Stewart, 1995, p.1). One international consortium which is coordinated by the Sanger Centre in Cambridge, UK at which the Resource Centre is located, includes laboratories at the Stanford University Genome Center, the Wellcome Trust Centre for Human Genetics in Oxford, Genethon in Paris, Washington University, the University of Cambridge (UK) and the Whitehead Institute/MIT in Cambridge, USA. It has now been accepted that developing a single, integrated database is unrealistic, and, as long as the connections are transparent for users, a set of databases may prove to be a richer resource.

## Changing the Funding Base

Human genome research in the UK, as already noted (OST, 1994), is mainly funded through the MRC and two charities, the Wellcome Trust and the Imperial Cancer Research Fund (ICRF). The BBSRC has responsibility for identifying genes controlling commercially important traits (such as growth and fertility) in animals and other species. It collaborates closely with the MRC on collaborative work. The Wellcome Trust has committed substantial funds to key centres in the Wellcome Trust Centre for Human Genetics, the Sanger Centre and the European Bioinformatics Institute in Cambridge. The ICRF has generated, via its funding of cancer research, a number of important resources including YAC and cDNA libraries. The significant role of the large charities cannot therefore be overlooked, although there is a degree of overlap in the key personnel sufficient to ensure a harmony of interests.

In addition, some funding is likely from the EC's new biomedicine and health research programme (Biomed 2). This is likely to allocate some 40 million ECUs to transnational genome research programmes in Europe in 1995/6. A significant change has also taken place in the nature of the funding from the MRC. Until 1994, applications for research in genome mapping were reviewed by the Directed Programme Committee. This allowed, as was noted above, some projects to be funded for their strategic value rather than their intrinsic scientific merit. The OST report stated that this "enabled projects to be considered expeditiously in keeping with the rapid advances in the field" (OST, 1994, p. 13). Now, however, funding applications are peer reviewed in the normal way, together with bids for other MRC resources, and the ring-fencing has been removed. The responsibility for advising on policy and identifying strategic areas for the future now rests with an overarching HGMP Coordinating Committee. This change does, however, make available the whole of the MRC's research budget against which to bid for HGMP funds.

One of the implications of these changes is the need to find other means by which the more routine aspects of sequencing can be funded. It is no longer possible to pass off mundane science as a strategic necessity, especially in a policy climate of innovation and wealth creation. This makes the development of large-scale laboratories such as the Sanger Institute in Cambridge, or Genethon in France, a necessary adjunct to relatively small, dispersed and networked groups of researchers. These laboratories are characterised by high levels of automation, and employ relatively few scientists compared to technicians, whose prime activity is to generate large quantities of genomic data (Thomas, 1994). In turn, the availability of these data is leading to efforts to create management systems to facilitate access to the integrated databases mentioned earlier.

## Conclusion

This chapter has explored a number of issues within the UK HGMP, including the processes of prioritisation of objectives, the linkages between individuals and organisations, the problems of coordination, and the changing bases for funding. In doing so it has used the MRC Resource Centre as an example of a form of scientific cooperation network, and shown how it has, through being flexible and progressive, developed many of the organisational mechanisms and cultural resources required to facilitate the continuing growth of genomic research in Britain.

The HGMP Resource Centre has now moved into Hinxton Hall, Cambridge, alongside the Wellcome-funded Sanger Centre. The subsequent changes in management and direction, combined with the proximity of a large centre for genomic research, and in the context of an MRC initiative on Genetic Approaches to Human Health, should ensure that it continues to develop. This suggests that the UK has moved significantly to resolve a major issue of management and organisation in biology by combining a significant central resource within a widely distributed heterogeneous network of large and small research groups, some of whom are only peripherally concerned with mapping the human genome.

## References

Anderson, C. (1991) US patent application stirs up gene hunters. *Nature*, **353**, 485-486.
Balmer, B. (1993) Mutations in the Research System? The Human Genome Project as Science Policy. Unpublished DPhil Thesis, University of Sussex.
Balmer, B. & Martin, B.R. (1991) Who's doing what in human genome research? *Scientometrics*, **22**, 3, 369-377.
Bates, C. (1992) A Report on the Quantitative Survey of Registered Users of the HGMP Resource Centre. Unpublished Report, HGMP Resource Centre, Harrow.
Bennett, D., Glasner, P. & Travis, D. (1986) *The Politics of Uncertainty: Regulating Recombinant DNA Research in Britain*. Routledge and Kegan Paul, London.
Bishop, J.E. & Waldholz, M. (1990) *Genome*. Touchston, Simon and Schuster, New York.
Bodmer, W.F. (1990) The Human Genome Organisation. *Biofutur, October*, 95-98.

Bud, R. (1994) The Uses of Life: A History of Biotechnology. Cambridge University Press, Cambridge.

Cambrosio, A. & Keating, P. (1988) 'Going monoclonal': art, science and magic in the day-to-day use of hybridoma technology. *Social Problems*, **35**, 244-260.

Davis, J. (1990) *Mapping the Code*. Wiley, New York.

Fujimura, J.H. (1987) Constructing the 'do-able' programs in cancer research: articulating alignment. *Social Studies of Science*, **17**, 257-293.

Genome Digest (1995) Green Light from the European Commission for all specific programmes of the Fourth RTD Framework Programme. *Genome Digest*, **2**, 11.

Gibson, K. (1995) Coordinating a YAC resource in Europe. *Genome Digest*, **2**, 12-13.

Hilgartner, S. (1994) The Human Genome Project. In Jasanoff, S., Markle, G.E., Petersen, J.C. & Pinch, T. (eds) *Handbook of Science and Technology Studies*. Sage, London.

HMSO (1993) *Realising our Potential-A Strategy for Science and Technology*, Cmnd 2250. HMSO, London.

Kevles, D.J. & Hood, L. (1992) *The Code of Codes*. Harvard University Press, Cambridge.

Law, J. (1987) Technology and heterogeneous engineering: the case of Portuguese expansion. In Weibe, W.E., Hughes, T.P. & Pinch, T. (eds) *The Social Construction of Technological Systems*. MIT Press, Cambridge, 111-134.

Macharzina, K. & Staehle, W.H. (1986) *European Approaches to International Management*. de Gruyter, Berlin.

Magnien, E., Bevan, M. & Kees, P. (1992) A European 'BRIDGE' project to tackle a model plant genome. *TIBTECH*, **10**, 12-15.

McCain, K.W. (1991) Communication, competition and secrecy: the production and dissemination of research-related information in genetics. *Science, Technology and Human Values*, **16**, 491-516.

McLaren, D.J. (1992) The human genome-UK and international research initiatives. *MRC News*.

Merton R.K. (1973) *The Sociology of Science*. University of Chicago Press, Chicago.

MRC (1991) The UK Human Genome Mapping Project. Project Manager's Report. Medical Research Council, London.

MRC (1992) MRC Review of the UK Human Genome Mapping Project. Project Manager's Report, Medical Research Council, London.

OST (1994) *The Human Genome Mapping Project in the UK. Priorities and Opportunities in Genome Research*. Office of Science and Technology, HMSO, London.

OTA (1988) *Mapping our Genes*. Office of Technology Assessment, Washington.

Ritter, O. (1995) IGD: comprehensive integration of human genome data and analytical tools. *Genome Digest*, **2**, 12-12.

Stars, S.L. & Ruhleder, K. (1994) Steps towards an ecology of infrastructure: complex problems in design and access for large-scale collaborative systems. *Computer Supported Cooperative Work (CSCW)*, **3**, 253-265.

Stewart, A. (1995) The human gene map initiative. *Genome Digest*, **2**, 1-4.

Thomas, S. (1994) Europe, the UK and Changing Institutions for Research: Molecular Genetics in Biotechnology. Unpublished paper given at the EASST Conference on Science, Technology and Change: New Theories, Realities, Institutions, Budapest, Hungary, 28-31 August.

Vassorotti, A. & Goffeau, A. (1992) Sequencing the yeast genome: the European effort. *TIBTECH*, **10**, 15-18.

Vinck, D., Kahana, B., Laredo, P. & Meter, J.B. (1993) A network approach to studying research programmes. *Technology Analysis and Strategic Management*, **5**, 39-54.

Webster, A. (1990) The incorporation of biotechnology into plant-breeding in Cambridge. In Varcoe, I., McNeill, M. & Yearley, S. (eds) *Deciphering Science and Technology*. Macmillan, London.

Webster, A. (1991) *Science, Technology and Society: New Directions*. Macmillan, London.

Yoxen, E. (1983) *The Gene Business*. Pan Books, London.

Ziman, J. (1987) *Science in a 'Steady State': The Research System in Transition*. SPSG, London.

# 6 Eugenics Here and Now

RUTH McNALLY

ABSTRACT    *This chapter identifies the recent emergence of a eugenic discourse which is having a profound effect on public expenditure, legal configurations, reproductive decisions and attitudes towards genetic illness and handicap in England. The practices legitimated by the discourse combine the social welfare and psychosocial elements of Osborn's eugenic hypothesis with neo-liberal individual responsibility. However while the discourse itself is eugenic, the practices it legitimates-including human genome research, the activities of the human genetics services and the operation of the law relating to termination of pregnancy for fetal handicap-fail to meet Galton's eugenic criteria because their humaneness is questionable and they are unlikely to lead to 'genetic improvement' of the human species.*

## Discursive Eugenics

Fifty years ago, the principal cause of morbidity and mortality was infectious disease but with the discovery of antibiotics and improvements in hygiene and pest control, it is now a minor one in industrialised countries. Apart from the consequences of accident or war, much disease today has a genetic component (CEC, 1988, p. 3).

In recent years, genetic illness and handicap appear to have been constructed as a new social problem-the 'genetic problem'. The above quote is from *Predictive Medicine,* the 1988 proposal of the Commission of the European Communities (CEC, 1988) for a programme of human genome research, but a similar argument can be found in many documents on modern human genetics. This is not to suggest that the problem of genetically caused illness and handicap did not exist previously, but that, in recent years, it has been rendered visible by being generalised and articulated as a social problem.

One way in which the genetic problem is expressed is in terms of harm and cost, that is, suffering to the affected individual, anxiety and hardship to carers and families, and economic costs to society:

The overall costs of genetic diseases to individuals, families, and society are incalculable. Families commonly experience unjustifiable guilt, which may result in divorce and neglect of the normal siblings. For society the predicted lifetime cost in 1982 for institutional and medical care for a single patient with trisomy 21 was one-third of a million pounds (Connor & Ferguson-Smith, 1987, p. 196).

(Single gene disorders) typically ... afflict babies and young people, causing physically and often mentally crippling symptoms (Watson *et al.*, N1983, p. 211).

The genetic problem is also given a size dimension:

At least 7.5% of all conceptions have a chromosomal abnormality ... Genetic disease now causes about one-half of all deaths in childhood and accounts for one-third of all paediatric hospital admissions. Between 0.3% and 0.4% of children are severely mentally retarded, with mild mental retardation in a further 3% and significant physical handicap in 1-2%. Most of this handicap is genetic in aetiology. Finally, chronic diseases with a significant genetic component affect about 10-20 of the adult population (Connor & Ferguson-Smith, 1987 pp. 197-198).

The boundaries of the genetic problem are significantly expanded by the use of 'risk'. For example, the Royal College of Physicians (RCP), emphasising 'reproductive risk', states that "Everyone is at risk for having abnormal offspring" (RCP, 1989, p. 1.) Everyone is, of course, at risk of having abnormal offspring, but only in the same way that everyone is at risk of being struck by lightning! Only 3% of couples have a high and recurrent risk of bearing a child with a specific inherited disorder. However, ignorance of individual reproductive risk does indeed place every pregnancy *at risk of being at risk:*

Most infants with congenital malformations and chromosomal disorders are born to healthy young women with no previously identifiable risk factors (RCP, 1989, p.11).

In addition to reproductive risks, there is 'risk of illness' through genetic susceptibility:

Many common and debilitating diseases such as coronary artery disease ... (result) from the exposure of genetically susceptible people to environmental factors (CEG, 1988, p. 1).

... As it is most unlikely that we will be able to remove completely the environmental risk factors, it is important that we learn as much as possible about genetically determined predisposing factors and hence identify high-risk individuals (CEC, 1988, p. 3).

From the concept of risk through genetic susceptibility, it follows that as-yet unidentified and presently healthy individuals are also part of the genetic problem. The inclusion of risk in the definition of the genetic problem increases its size because, defined in this way, the problem also affects those who are currently unharmed, but are at risk of harm in the future. When the problem is expressed in terms of 'reproductive risk' it embraces the entire reproductive population. When expressed in terms of 'risk of illness', it tends towards the inclusion of almost every citizen. The net result is that almost the entire population in advanced industrial societies is given the status of either being part of, or being at risk from the genetic problem.

Typically, a constructed social problem has constructed 'solutions' and the genetic problem is no exception. One solution, proposed by the CEC and others, is research on the human genome:

> *Predictive medicine* seeks to protect individuals from the kinds of illnesses to which they are genetically most vulnerable and, where appropriate, to prevent the transmission of the genetic susceptibilities to the next generation (CEC, 1988, p. 3).

The CEC's genome research programmes are among a number of national and international projects (STOA, 1992) aiming to map and sequence the human genome. In 1989, the CEC allocated 15 million ECU to human genome research for the period 1989-1990. A further 27.5 million ECU was allocated for the period 1990-1994 and 40.32 million ECU for the period 1994-1998.

While the CEC proposes human genome research as a solution to the genetic problem, the RCP argues for the expansion of clinical and community genetics services (human genetics services):

> Genetic counselling, the detection of carriers, and the prenatal diagnosis that is available for many diseases (and in particular for the most common), as well as relieving the burden to families and carers, will lead to such a reduction in birth frequency of serious abnormalities that the savings to the NHS outweigh the expenses of the services (RCP, 1991, p. 1).

A key practice of the human genetics services is prenatal testing:

> Many of the couples with a high risk can be enabled to have healthy children through the application of prenatal tests (RCP, 1991, p. 4).

> (Prenatal testing provides) reassurance when the foetus is unaffected, and information, prognosis and choice, when a severe abnormality is present (RCP, 1989, p. 51).

In a minority of cases, a prenatal test result which indicates that the fetus has an abnormality can result in a healthy baby through therapy. However, in the majority of cases the choice provided by a positive prenatal test result is whether or not to terminate the pregnancy:

> Most of those at risk for severe disease choose to terminate the pregnancy, and soon undertake another in the hope of replacing the aborted foetus with a healthy one (RCP, 1989, p. 40).

Termination of pregnancy on the grounds of fetal handicap is lawful in England, Scotland and Wales subject to provisions under Section (1) (1) (d) of the (amended) Abortion Act 1967. Under this Act:

> A person shall not be guilty of an offence when a pregnancy is terminated by a registered medical practitioner if two registered medical practitioners are of the opinion, formed in good faith ... that there is a substantial risk that if the child were born it would suffer from such physical or mental abnormalities as to be seriously handicapped.

In 1990, the Abortion Act was amended by the Human Fertilisation and Embryology (HFE) Act, so that there is no longer an upper time limit on such terminations.

If the human genome research programme seems ambitious; the proposals for the human genetics services are no less so. In addition to arguing for the routine screening of the entire pregnant population, the RCP also advocates screening the entire reproductive population for carriers of certain genetic traits.

The above account of the construction of the genetic problem and its solution is a linear and causal account. It starts with the construction of the genetic problem and is followed by the articulation of solutions which are supposed to ameliorate the problem. However, there are alternative 'histories of the present' which problematise this account.

For example, why has something which is constitutive of what it is to be human - the human genome - has been constructed as the cause of a social problem in advanced industrial countries in very recent times? Genetic disease and handicap affect all populations and have been apparent since prehistory. The infant mortality rate (number of babies dying during the first year of life per 1000 live-births) due to genetic disease in England and Wales is 4.5/1000 and has not altered since 1900. Moreover, the same pattern is apparent for fetal wastage and also for diseases of later childhood and adult life (Connor & Ferguson-Smith, 1987).

One reason for the recent construction of the genetic problem in advanced industrial countries is its increased relative importance due to the declining importance of infectious diseases. However, this change has been a steady trend over the past 50 years, rather than a recent discontinuity. The picture is, however, dramatically different if one reverses the question and looks for a discontinuity of solutions, rather than of problems.

Genetics is a twentieth century science. Almost since its inception there have been attempts to map genes on to chromosomes, and the idea of mapping the entire human genome predated the technical means to achieve it. However, recent years have witnessed what Professor David Weatherall has described as a molecular 'revolution in the biological sciences' (1985, p. 587). This revolution is marked by the advent of recombinant DNA (rDNA) technology - a new set of techniques developed in the early 1970s which enables genetic engineers to decode, compare, construct, mutate, excise, join, transfer and clone specific sequences of DNA through 'micogenetic engineering' (see Wheale & McNally, 1986, 1988). Thus, while as described above, there is no obvious recent discontinuity in the incidence of genetic illness or handicap, the advent of DNA technology in the early 1970s and its application in the 1980s is a recent event which could be a factor in the recent construction of the genetic problem.

Documentary analysis indicates that the very existence of rDNA technology is used to justify human genome research. For example, the CEC writes: "... there was no way of locating genes whose product was unknown until, in the 1970s, recombinant DNA technology provided a new approach" (CEC, 1988, p 6).

Genome research is also funded as part of a strategy to improve economic growth and international competitiveness. For example, in his Presidential address to the British Association for the Advancement of Science (BAAS) Meeting in 1988, Sir Walter Bodmer announced that human genome research will create the 'handbook of man', which will provide the basis for the prevention or treatment of most major human chronic disease, and will stimulate technological developments that are certain to be of considerable economic benefit. Indeed, one-fifth of the budget requested under the proposal for predictive medicine was for research to improve advanced genetic technologies. Also, the evaluative criteria for the programme are the number of gene probes developed, gene libraries established, scientists trained and research networks formed rather than reduction in the size of the genetic problem.

Many descriptions of genome research treat it as an 'international race', in particular between the European Union (EU), the US and Japan. However, what will mark its endpoint? Will genome research end (if it ever does) when the genome runs out or when the money runs out? Either way, it is unlikely to be ended because the genetic problem research effectively increases the size of the genetic problem through the 'geneticisation' (Lippman, 1994) of multi-factorial diseases for which there is scant or no genetic evidence. An example of this would be claims for genetic linkage in homosexuality and criminality. Such research not only renders these behaviours as part of the genetic problem, but the very refutation of such claims sustains the demand for further genetic research to establish their 'truth' or otherwise.

Thus, the different rationalities for allocating resources to genome research intensify each other: the genetic problem justifies research on the human genome, which justifies the development of more technology, which justifies more genome research, which expands the genetic problem. What unites these rationalities is the legitimacy of the science of genetics.

The knowledge constructed from human genome research is biometric; it comprises new measurements of population norms and deviations, information which constitutes a new system of classification, new definitions of normal and abnormal and new ways of distinguishing them from each other (McNally & Wheale, 1994; Wheale & McNally, 1994). Indeed, the desire to be able to distinguish between the normal and the abnormal was one of the justifications of the scientific content of the CEC's proposed human genome research programme:

> ... the ability to understand normal gene functions, and hence to recognise the
> abnormal and then predict disease susceptibility, rests on having access to a
> 'human gene dictionary' (CEC, 1988, p. 13).

The knowledge deriving from human genome research increases the 'need' for human genetics services:

> The needs of the population for genetic services have increased because for many
> genetic disorders it is now possible to identify carriers of genetic disease and to
> make a diagnosis before birth (RCP, 1991, p. 2).

Formerly, only about 120 pregnancies per year in the UK were at risk for ... prenatally diagnosable inborn errors of metabolism, but this number has trebled now that prenatal diagnosis for cystic fibrosis is available (Connor & Ferguson-Smith, 1987, p. 197).

Similarly, the very use of human genetics services creates the 'need' for more human genetics services, manifested in the expanding array of human genetic professions and their institutional infrastructures which support and administer those who are going to be, or have been, in receipt of genetic information. These professions include genetic nurses, genetic midwives, genetic counsellors, genetic social works and genetic psychiatrists.

A new network of expertise involving the scientific, medical, social work, educational and legal systems is developing as a result of the self-sustaining, ever-expanding cycle of new knowledge, new techniques, new systems of classification, new vocabularies, new professions, and professional specialisations and new organisational structures. This new network is based upon the use of genetics as a science, a technology, a system of classification, a social problem and a solution to that problem.

Figure 1 is a model proposed by the RCP (1989) as the ideal type of human genetic services at the district health authority level. At the centre of the model is the reproductive couple; however, many of the services are primarily targeted at pregnant women and their fetuses, and these will be the focus of the following sections.

## The Eugenic Hypothesis

In the late 1930s, Frederic Osborn proposed the 'eugenic hypothesis', as an example of a eugenics programme which is designed to work within the framework of a social welfare democracy. Under such circumstances, Osborn believed, there would be no need for a Eugenic Board of Control. "The environment, according to Osborn, could be designed to generate eugenic selection, and the individual might not even be conscious of the fact that he or she was under 'pressure' to reproduce or not to reproduce" (Bajema, 1976, p. 269). This would be achieved through "the introduction of measures of a psychological and cultural sort" (Osborn, 1940, p. 198).

The social milieu in the England at the present time combine the social welfare and psychosocial elements of Osborn's eugenic hypothesis with neo-liberal individual responsibility. Firstly, with regard to social welfare, both public funding of human genome research and publicly funded human genetics services exist.

Secondly, with regard to measures of a 'psychological and cultural sort', there is a discourse on healthy babies and reproductive choice which may normalise pregnant women to undergo prenatal diagnosis and pregnancy termination. There is also legal provision for the termination of pregnancy for fetal handicap, and 'wrongful birth' actions. Under English case law on 'wrongful birth' *(McKay v Essex Area Health Authority)*, the human genetics services are under a duty to advise potential parents of the risks of illness or handicap in any future offspring, and to carry out diagnostic procedures in order to establish abnormalities, in existing foetuses *in utero* (Fortin, 1987, p. 306). In addition, if it can be reasonably foreseen that the pregnant woman may bear a disabled child, the medical advice should include information that this risk would make an abortion legally justified. Negligence in respect of any of these duties could be the basis of a claim for wrongful birth.

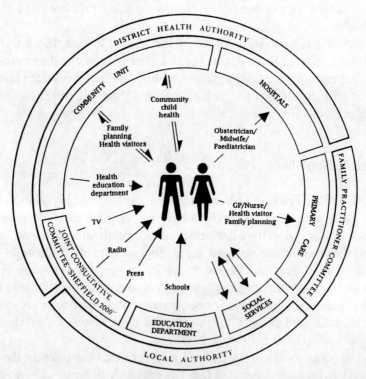

**Figure 1.** A couple at reproductive risk in the mist of human genetic services.
*Source:* RCP (1989, p. 9).

As with any medical procedure, the consent of the pregnant woman is a necessary condition for the termination of pregnancy. While this gives her autonomy, it also makes her, rather than the policies and practices which provide her with this option, responsible for the outcome of her decision, whether it is the birth of an affected child or the termination of the pregnancy.

Common reactions of women and their partners following termination of pregnancy for fetal handicap are shock, confusion disbelief, grief and anxiety (SATFA, 1992, p. 8). "In contrast to the mostly positive reactions of women after an abortion for psychosocial indications, many authors (herself included) have observed the opposite following a termination for fetal abnormality" (White-van Mourik, 1994, p. 116). What makes such terminations different from terminations for psychosocial indications is that, in almost all cases, the pregnancies which are terminated under the fetal handicap ground are wanted pregnancies, and the woman has to come to terms with the euthanasia of her own child because of the risk that it was going to be handicapped.

Choice and responsibility are two sides of the same coin. The pregnant woman's option not to be informed, and hence not to have to choose whether or not to terminate, is diminishing. This is because human genome research is expanding the choices. Case law on wrongful birth places the genetics services under a duty to bring reproductive choices to the pregnant woman's notice; and the normative discourse on parental responsibility to have healthy babies through reproductive choice is clamouring.

## Eugenic Practices?

Man is gifted with pity and other kindly feelings; he has also the power of preventing many kinds of suffering. I conceive it to fall well within his province to replace Natural Selection by other processes that are more merciful and not less effective. This is precisely the aim of Eugenics (Galton, 1908, p. 323).

The word 'eugenics' was coined in 1883 by Sir Francis Galton, the cousin of Charles Darwin. According to Galton, proposals, policies or practices are eugenic if they modify natural selection in a humane way and lead to genetic improvement of the human species. The inhuman practices of Nazi Germany fail both of Galton's criteria, and thus cannot be called eugenic (Bajema, 1976). However, are the proposals, policies and practices currently in operation in England eugenic by Galton's criteria?

Potential eugenic policies and practices include:

- publicly funded research on the human genome which (among other things) generates new public diagnostic tests;
- a publicly funded human genetics service which (among other things) undertakes genetic diagnosis; and
- legal provision for the termination of pregnancy on the grounds of (among other things) genetic diagnosis.

The first criterion I shall consider is the potential of such activities to lead to 'genetic improvement'. From a discursive perspective, this could be an expectation. As described above, public expenditure on human genome research is, in part, legitimated by its potential to prevent the transmission of genetic susceptibility. Similarly, the provision of human genetics services by the state is also premised on its potential to reduce the birth frequency of serious abnormalities. However, as will be argued below, there may be a difference between the legitimating eugenic discourse on these practices and their effects.

'Genetic improvement' of the human species is a loaded term, but interpreting it modestly as the elimination of genetic determinants for illness and handicap, it can be said that the termination of pregnancy for an abnormality which is not genetic is not a eugenic practice; neither is abortion a eugenic necessity when the genetic handicap or illness is such that the affected person is not biologically 'fit', that is, will not reproduce, for example through sterility or death in childhood. For conditions determined by a single dominant gene, abortion of the affected fetus is eugenic because it eliminates the responsible gene. However, as calculated by Professor R.C. Punnet in 1917, for autosomal, recessive, single-gene disorders, the large majority of the responsible genes in a population will be present as a single copy in unaffected individuals known as carriers, rather than in affected individuals (homozygotes) who have inherited one copy of the gene from each parent. Although the carriers of most single-gene disorders suffer no ill effects from their carrier status, the prevention of their birth would be eugenic because it would eliminate the genetic determinant from the population. However, there is no legal provision for termination when the only risk is that the fetus is a carrier. (A policy of termination for carrier status would threaten the very existence of the species given that every human carries between three and eight genes for lethal, recessive disorders.)

On the other hand, to reduce the frequency of a gene responsible for an autosomal recessive condition from 1/100 to 1/1 000 000 by selection against homozygotes (for example, through the termination of pregnancies of affected fetuses) would take 684 generations (in humans, approximately 1700 years) (Punnet, 1917). Moreover, the prevention of the birth of homezygotes through abortion increases the probability of the birth of a carrier child born to carrier couples from 1/2 to 2/3. Thus, abortion of homozygous fetuses with recessive conditions is not only of limited potential with respect to the 'genetic improvement' of the population, it may also be dysgenic.

Galton's second eugenic criterion is that proposals, policies and practices should be humane. Termination of pregnancy is one of the most contentious areas in law, and remains high on the political agenda precisely because it almost always results in the death of the fetus. The direct link between prenatal testing and termination of pregnancy has not gone unnoticed by the Catholic church:

> All parents should know the purpose of the tests being offered to the pregnant mother. ... She might discover that a particular test is being proposed because it is taken for granted that she would not wish to keep her child if it were found to be suffering from a handicap. Many doctors and midwives today are willing to help a mother obtain an abortion, if her child is suffering from Down's syndrome (mongolism), spina bifida (a defect of the backbone or spine), or a genetic illness such as cystic fibrosis, sickle cell disease or other severe blood disorders (Catholic Bishop's Joint Committee on Bio-ethical Issues, 1989, pp. 3-4).

Notwithstanding such concerns, the fetal handicap ground was considered to be one of the more socially accepted grounds for the termination of pregnancy during the parliamentary debates on the amendment of the Abortion Act under the HFE Act (Morgan & Lee, 1991). Crucial to its acceptability is the interpretation of its main purpose (Morgan, 1990). Is it so that the pregnant woman can protect her interests, is it to serve the economic interests of the state, or it is to protect the interests of the fetus?

For some, the 'economic burden on society' interpretation is unpalatable because of its utilitarian attitude towards future citizens. For others, the 'pregnant woman's interests' interpretation is also unacceptable because it endorses the rejection of handicapped children. Such terminations may be rendered more acceptable if utilitarianism is fused with humanitarian consideration of fetal interests (Wheale & McNally, 1988, p. 270). For example, SATFA, the charity for support after termination for abnormality, states that: "The decision to terminate a wanted baby because of foetal abnormality is one made out of care for the unborn child" (SATFA, 1992, p. 1). Similarly, Lord Justice Stephenson interpreted the fetal handicap ground in the Abortion Act of 1967 as follows:

that paragraph may have been passed in the interests of the mother, the family and the general public, but I would prefer to believe that its main purpose, if not its sole purpose, was to benefit the unborn child (*McKay v. Essex Area Health Authority* at 780).

Therefore, termination of pregnancy, which is a violation of the principle of the sanctity of the life of the fetus, may be morally justified within an ethical framework of humanitarian utilitarianism which construes this action as being in the interests of the foetus itself.

One problem with such a 'humane' interpretation of the fetal handicap ground is that the risk which legitimates the termination may be to the pregnancy in general, rather than to a particular fetus. For example, in X-linked recessive conditions where the mother is a carrier, the laws of Mendelian inheritance predict that 50% of male fetuses will be normal and 50% will be affected, while female fetuses will be either carriers of normal. For such conditions where there is no specific prenatal diagnostic test, all male fetuses may be aborted to avoid the risk of the birth of an affected child. However, on average 50% of the aborted fetuses will be normal. For such fetuses, it is hard to argue that the termination was in their interests. To a lesser degree, this is the case even when there is a specific prenatal test; the result of many such tests is probabilistic, and the decision to terminate, and indeed the legal provision for termination, is based on an estimate of risk, rather than proof, that the fetus is affected. Furthermore, even when the fetus is affected, it can be problematic to argue that the termination of its only potential for existence is in its interests, particularly in conditions like Huntington's disease, where onset usually occurs in adulthood.

The fetal interests interpretation also become problematic when taken to its logical conclusion. If the fetal handicap ground exists because it is in the interests of fetuses that pregnancies which meet its criteria be terminated, then it could be argued that there should be a reciprocal duty to terminate all pregnancies which meet these criteria in order that the interests of all such fetuses might be upheld.

However, no one is under a duty to terminate a pregnancy in the interests of a fetus. Indeed, English case law (*McKay v Essex Area Health Authority*) on 'wrongful life' is that a child whose pregnancy could have been lawfully terminated under the fetal handicapground has no legal 'cause of action' for negligence against others for having failed to have acted in his or her interests prior to birth by not diagnosing the condition and terminating the pregnancy. The diagnosis that there is a substantial risk that her child will be seriously handicapped furnishes the pregnant woman with the option of pregnancy termination, but does not place a duty on any party to terminate the pregnancy in the fetus's interests. Thus, while the termination of pregnancy for fetal handicap may be discursively formulated as being a humane act undertaken in the fetus's (or unborn child's ) interests, in practice this in only the case when those interests coincide with those of other parties, especially those of the pregnant women.

In summary, the discourse which legitimates the proposals, practices and policies embodied in human genome research, the human genetics services, and the fetal handicap ground for abortion is eugenic. However, the extent to which the practices and policies themselves meet Galton's eugenic criteria is questionable, both in the extent to which they are humane and with respect to their potential to 'improve' the genetic constitution of the human species. However, this does not mean that the eugenic discourse which legitimates these practices is not having a profound effect on public expenditure, legal configurations, reproductive decisions and attitudes towards genetic illness and handicap.

**References**

Bajema, C.J. (1976) *Eugenics Then and Now.* Dowden, Hutchinson and Ross, Stroundsburg, PA, USA.

Catholic Bishops' Joint Committee on Bio-ethical Issues (1989) *Antenatal Tests: What You Should Know.* Catholic Truth Society, London.

CEC (1988) *Proposal for a Council Decision Adopting a Specific Research Programme in the Field of Health: Predictive Medicine: Human Genome Analysis (1989-1990).* COM(88) 424 final-SYN 146, 20 July, Brussels.

Connor, J.M. & Ferguson-Smith, M.A. (1987) *Essential Medical Genetics.* Blackwell Scientific, Oxford.

Fortin, J.E.S. (1987) Is the 'wrongful life' action really dead? *Journal of Social Welfare Law,* 306-313.

Galton, F. (1908) *Memories of My Life.* Methuen, London.

Lippman, A. (1994) Prenatal genetic testing and screening: constructing needs and reinforcing inequitities. In Clark, A. (ed.) *Genetic Counselling: Practice and Principles.* Routledge, London 143-186.

*McKay v. Essex Area Health Authority (1982) 2 All ER 771.*

McNally, R.M. & Wheale, P.R. (1994) Environmental and medical bioethics in late modernity: Anthony Giddens, genetic engineering and the post-modern state. In Attfield, R. & Belsey, A. (eds) *Philosophy and the Natural Environment,* Cambridge University Press, Cambridge, 211-226.

Morgan, D. (1990) Abortion: the unexamined ground. *Criminal Law Review,* 687-694.

Morgan, D. & Lee, R.G. (1991) *Blackstone's Guide to the Human Fertilisation and Embryology Act 1990: Abortion and Embryo Research, The New Law*. Blackstone Press, London.

Osborn, F. (1940) *Preface to Eugenics*. Harper and Row, New York, NY, USA.

Punnet, R.C. (1917) Eliminating feeblemindedness. *Journal of Heredity*, **8**, 464-465.

RCP (1989) *Prenatal Diagnosis and Genetic Screening: Community and Service Implications*. Royal College of Physicians, London, September.

RCP (1991) *Purchasers' Guidlines to Genetic Services in the NHS: An Aid to Assessing the Genetic Services Required by the Resident Population of an Average Health District; Report of a Working Group of the Clinical Genetics Committee of the Royal College of Physicians*. Royal College of Physicians, London, October.

SATFA (1992) *SATFA News*, September.

STOA (1992) *Bioethics in Europe: Final Report*. European Parliament DG IV, Luxembourg.

Watson, J.D., Tooze, J. & Kurtz, D. (1983) *Recombinant DNA: A Short Course*. Freeman, New York, NY, USA.

Weatherall, D.J. (1985) *The New Genetics and Clinical Practice*. Oxford University Press, Oxford.

Wheale, P.R. & McNally, R.M. (1986) Patent trend analysis: the case of genetic engineering. *Futures*, October, 638-657.

Wheale, P.R. & McNally, R.M. (1988) *Genetic Engineering: Catastrophe or Utopia?* Wheatsheaf, Hemel Hempstead.

Wheale, P.R. & McNally, R.M. (1994) What bugs genetic engineers about bioethics. In Dyson, A. & Harris, J. (eds) *Ethics and Biotechnology*. Routledge, London, 179-201.

White-van Mourik, M. (1994) Termination of a second-trimester pregnancy for fetal abnormality: psychosocial aspects. In Vlarke, A. (ed.) *Genetic Counselling: Practice and Principles*. Routledge, London, 113-132.

# 7 Moral and Legal Consequences for the Fetus/Unborn Child of Medical Technologies Derived from Human Genome Research

PETER R. WHEALE

ABSTRACT    *Human genome research is providing knowledge of the genetic determination of genetically based diseases and disorders and is facilitating the development of new reproductive technologies. This chapter explores the moral and legal status of the fetus and the child prior to its birth, and attempts to reveal the ethical and legal principles and underpinning the medico-legal practices of embryo research, genetic screening and abortion. The author reveals legal contradictions and tensions between English common law (underpinned by the sanctity of life principle) and civil law (supported by utilitarian values). Invoking Rawls' moral theorising in* A Theory of Justice, *the author argues that these contradictions are producing a 'reflective disequilibrium', which, he concludes, could even bring medical law into disrepute.*

## Introduction

One of the stated objectives of human genome research (COM(88) 424 final-SYN 146) is to provide scientific knowledge of the genetic determination of disease and genetic predispositions to disorders, and to develop technologies to prevent the inheritance of such diseases and disorders. These medical technologies focus attention on reproduction, and have generated discourses on the moral and legal status of the fetus.

In this chapter, I explore the controversy surrounding the discourse on the question of when human life is deemed to have gained moral and legal personality. The ethics implied by the medical use of embryos for research purposes are considered, and the ethico-legal underpinnings of the legal termination of pregnancy are explored. The analysis focuses on the contradictions between English common law, which embodies the sanctity of life principle - the basic

83

principle which places upon us the moral duty not to kill innocent human beings - and English civil law which, I argue, is largely supported by utilitarian values.

Central to my analysis is the idea that a form of utilitarianism, based on 'quality of life' values, is embedded in these new technologies. I suggest, therefore, that utilitarian values are displacing the sanctity of life principle and creating a 'reflective disequilibrium', the opposite of 'reflective equilibrium' in the sense in which John Rawls uses the term (Rawls, 1972), and which is manifest in certain legal inconsistencies and ambiguities. This is particularly visible when we contrast the legal status of the viable (or 'normal') fetus with that of its seriously handicapped counterpart. Finally, I conclude that the ethico-legal contradictions, which together have created this 'reflective disequilibrium', could even bring medical law into disrepute.

## Moral Personality

Arguments persists over the question of at what point in time human life is deemed to have gained a moral personality and what criteria should be used to address this question. Grobstein (1981), for example, suggests physiological criteria should be used for recognising personhood. Such criteria include response to external change, the presence of a nervous system and the capacity to be recognised as human by others. This had led him to conclude that the state of personhood is reached by the end of the first trimester of pregnancy. Another widely held view (see, for example, Glover, 1990) is that the boundary of personhood should be 'viability', by which is usually meant physical independence of others. Yet others argue (see, for example, Hare, 1988) that even the earliest form of human life is potentially a person, and therefore should be entitled to full personhood rights.

The potentiality argument does not suggest that an individual already exists for whom the development of this potential constitutes a benefit (in this sense, gametes and embryos do not, as such, have interests), but that by its development it will derive future benefit as a grown person. The implication of the potentiality argument is that the interests of potential persons imposes on us a duty to preserve them. If we were to accept this argument, then we must concede that embryo research (which is non-therapeutic), abortion of healthy fetuses and infanticide are all morally wrong.

It follows from this that the duties of the moral agents, for example doctors and parents, towards the embryo derive from the fact that their actions may further, or impede, the coming into being of the child. However, severely handicapped fetuses may be excluded from this moral duty. Hare (1988) suggests that there is no duty to preserve handicapped fetuses and infants where the child is so handicapped that parents think it would be better to give the love to another future and more fortunate child.

Whereas the duty-based moralist would appraise an action intrinsically in terms of its moral character, the utilitarian appraises it extrinsically, that is, in terms of its consequences. This approach presents a strong challenge to the potentiality argument. Harris (1985), for example, challenges the potentiality argument by suggesting that we have no reason to treat a potential person in the same way as an actual person, and asserts that fetuses have no rights because the fetus is not a person and therefore cannot be wronged if its life is ended prematurely (for a contrary view, however, see, for example, Strong, 1991). In an attempt to reveal the absurdity of the potentiality argument, Harris also argues that "The unfertilised egg and the sperm are equally potentially new human beings" (Harris, 1985, p. 11).

Similarly, Glover (1990, Chapter 7), another utilitarian thinker, suggests that it is hard to see how the potentiality argument can succeed against abortion without also succeeding against contraception. Both involve the prevention of somebody coming into existence in whose interest it almost certainly was to exist (Glover, 1990, p. 122). However, few wish to argue that contraception is on a par with abortion, or that sperm should be treated with the same respect that we treat the neonate.

In Kant's (1948) *Groundwork of the Metaphysic of Morals,* his second formulation of the Categorical Imperative enjoins us to treat people always as ends and never 'merely as means'. However, he denies moral consideration to non-rational beings, for example, non-human animals: the individual's right to equal respect is the right of individuals to have respect for their intrinsic purpose, and, in his view, non-rational beings do not have any. Following this line of argument, Tooley (1972) is of the opinion that rationality and self-awareness, "the concept of self as a continuing subject of experiences and other mental states", are the determining factors for personhood. Rawls' (1972, p. 512) notion of contractualism - which is a duty-based system of values attempting to ground principles of morality in some hypothetical procedure of collective choice - is also conditional upon this sort of 'rational egotism'.

Does the logic of the rational egoists' argument mean, however, that embryos and fetuses, as non-rational agents, may be used 'merely as a means' to an end without transgressing Kantian morality? The answer to this question must depend on whether we regard rationality as a necessary condition for personhood status, or merely a sufficient condition. Just as the fetus is not a rational agent, it can be argued that neither are very young children or severely mentally handicapped adults, but this does not mean that we cannot (and, in fact, we do) accord them rights. That an 'incompetent' adult is unable to claim a right does not necessarily destroy that individual's right (the rights being endorsed may be 'natural' rights, 'human' rights, universally valid or individually based; see, for example, Macfarlane, 1990).

It seems clear that a simple rational egoist' position is contrary to any civilised society's moral intuitions - its consequences are often to violate what Griffin (1992) calls the principle of 'psychological realism'. It is also contrary to Rawls' (1972) theory of 'reflective equilibrium' - the notion whereby any theory of morals must accommodate the community's dominant moral intuitions, or be itself so persuasive that upon reflection the community is moved to abandon those intuitions which are incompatible with it. The inconsistency arises because such a moral position cannot accommodate the dominant intuition which does attribute a degree of moral status to individuals who are not autonomous, and therefore not capable of reciprocal contractual relationships.

Rawls (1972, p. 209) avoids the logic of his 'rational egoist' position by arguing that, in order to maintain the integrity of incompetent persons, we should act towards them as we have reason to believe they would choose for themselves if they were capable of reason and deciding rationally. Kant, on the other hand, attempts to avoid the logic of his rational agent thesis by asserting that we all owe a universal (indirect) duty to humanity. This follows from the first formulation of his Categorical Imperative, that is, to so act that your action can be willed without contradiction as a universal law. If we accept this universal duty, then 'incompetent' (non-rational) beings can be attributed with personhood status (Kant, 1948).

Following this same logic, however, why may we not attribute personhood status to the fetus? If we believe that the fetus has its own 'intrinsic' value, that is, that it has a 'good' of itself, then it would be regarded as morally 'considerable', and moral agents (for example doctors and parents) could have a (special) moral duty towards it. If we accept that a duty of care is due to the fetus, then it is surely but a small step to accord it related rights, as, for example, Kennedy (1988, Chapter 6) asserts that it should be. However, if the embryo was attributed with individual personhood rights, it becomes morally impermissible to use it merely instrumentally, for instance for scientific research. Such an assertion of the sanctity of life principle sharply conflicts with the utilitarian approach towards the fetus. The difficulty is that equal respect for individual rights is incompatible with utilitarian calculations of moral prudence.

## Legal Personality

In *R v. Tait* (1989), discussing the Offences Against the Person Act 1861, Section 16 (which provides that it is an offence without lawful excuse to make to another a threat, intending that other would fear it would be carried out, to kill that other or a third person), it was held that a fetus is not a 'third person'. Also, in *Paton v.Trustees of British Pregnancy Advisory Service* (1989), the plaintiff, a husband who wish to prevent his wife from having an abortion, was unsuccessful, and in *C v. S* (1988), a putative father of a fetus failed to obtain an injunction to prevent his girlfriend from having an abortion. These decisions restated the dictum of Baker P. (in *C v. S*, 1988, p. 1289) that "The foetus cannot, in English law ... have any right of its own at least until it is born and has a separate existence from the mother".

In *D v. Berkshire CC* (1987), events occurring prior to a child's birth were taken into account by the court when considering a post-natal 'care order' under Section 1 (2) (a) of the Children and Young Persons Act 1969; however, the care order was justified because the court was satisfied that, by reason of the mother's continuing behaviour, the child's post-natal development would continue to be avoidably prevented; and in *Re F (in utero,* 1988) the court of appeal dismissed an appeal against the refusal of a judge to make the unborn child (at term) of a mentally disturbed woman a ward of court, thus endorsing the lack of legal personhood for the fetus.

The 'wardship cases' referred to above, thus indicate the apparent improbability of any third party obtaining *locus standi* to intervene on behalf of the fetus, and reinforce the fact that, in English law, the unborn child has no legal status which can be enforced by a 'next friend', i.e. it has no legal personality. However, in the controversial case of *Re S* (Adult: Refusal of Treatment, 1992), in a remarkable application of the sanctity of life principle, and apparently contrary to this principle, the health authority in question applied to the high court for a declaration authorising the surgeons and hospital staff to carry out an emergency caesarean section operation on a 30-year old pregnant woman, despite the fact that she refused to give her consent to the operation. In granting the declaration, Sir Stephen Brown P declared that the caesarean section operation was "in the vital interests of the patient and the unborn child" and that it could be lawfully performed by the hospital staff despite S's refusal to give her consent.

The court's declaration in *Re S* effectively allowed the health authority to act in *locus standi* for the unborn child, and therefore appears to enhance the legal status of the unborn child. It reinforces legal arguments which allow increased wight to the interests of the viable fetus *vis-à-vis* the mother's rights to refuse treatment and retain bodily inviolability.  If established as a precedent *Re S* would have important implications for whether or not it can be lawful for a doctor to override a competent patient's refusal of consent to life-sustaining treatment in order to bring her viable fetus to term.

Turning to the English civil law, the Congenital Disabilities (Civil Liability) Act 1976 (CDCLA), however, states that a mother cannot be liable for negligence to her own fetus, thus ruling out pre-natal maternal tortious liability. The exception is where injuries are sustained as a result of a motor accident under Section 2 of the CDCLA, which specifically makes provision for maternal liability in respect of driving a motor vehicle.  It seems inconsistent for the law to recognise a maternal duty to a legal non-entity for injuries pre-natally caused as a result of negligent driving on the one hand, but not for maternal antenatal neglect (for example, conducting a life-style which causes injury to the child) on the other.

This maternal duty of care under Section 2 of the CDCLA does not apply, however, if the fetus is already seriously handicapped, as the mother of a handicapped child is exempt from liability under the Act for  pre-natal harm caused to the child (cf. Section 2).  This shows that the civil law clearly embodies a diminished status for the severely handicapped fetus relative to a 'normally' health one.

When a child or some agent acting on behalf of the child claims that it would have been best for that child never to have been born at all, and that but for the negligent actions of others who owed that child a duty of care that the child would not have been so born, then such a cause of action is called 'wrongful life'. In *McKay v. Essex Area Health Authority* (1982) a 'wrongful life' action was brought on behalf of Mrs McKay's daughter, claiming that, but for the negligence of her mother's doctor in not advising that she was at risk of conceiving a severely defective child, her mother would have either never have conceived her, or, having conceived her, would have elected to abort the fetus before term.  She would, therefore, never have been born at all (Law Commission, 1974).

The claim for 'wrongful life' in *McKay* failed because it was held that there is no duty to a child to abort a fetus.  In dismissing the plaintiff's claim, the court of appeal rejected the whole idea of a 'wrongful life' cause of action on the basis that it would be against public policy to argue that the life of the severely handicapped child was of no value, and that it should be compensated for its very existence (Whitefield, 1993).

This common law position contrasts markedly with the civil law in England.  The CDCLA 1976 confirms the existence of civil liability for pre-natal injuries causing disability (Section 1 (1) and 2 (a)).  Subject to certain defences (see Report on Injuries to Unborn Children, 1974) a child has a cause of action in respect of injuries sustained prior to its birth, providing it is born alive, as a result of the wrongful act of a person other than the child's own mother. Section 1 A (1) of the CDCLA 1976 (introduced by Section 44 of the Human Fertilisation and Embryology Act (HUFEA) to cover certain negligent conduct in relation to infertility treatments) provides that where, but for the negligence in the selection or storage of the embryo, a disabled child would not have been born, then the child's disabilities are to be regarded as damage resulting from the wrongful act of that person and actionable accordingly at the suit of the child unless the parents already knew of the risk (this breaks the chain of causation). Section 4(4) of the Act provides that for an action to lie, the child must be born and live for at least 48 h.

Section 1 A (1) of the CDCLA provides that a child has a claim against its father where the child's disabilities arise from his negligence in providing damaged sperm. Section 1 (3) of the CDCLA states that " ... it is no answer that there could not have been such liability because the parent suffered no actionable injury, if there could not have been such liability because the parent suffered no actionable injury, if there was a breach of legal duty which, accompanied by injury, would have given rise to the liability". The law is clear that, but for the negligence in giving sperm, that child would never have been born at all, and therefore it may be argued that the disabled child proving negligence but for which she would never have been born at all has a 'wrongful life' action, in marked contrast to the English common law where, as discussed above, 'wrongful life' actions are not recognised.

## Embryo Research

The argument that the benefit to a childless, infertile couple of having children is greater than the harm suffered by 'spare' embryos is essentially utilitarian. However, for the duty-based moralist (the deontologist), nothing morally impermissible can be made good by its consequences, and therefore nothing morally good can come of 'evil' (STOA, 1992).

The Committee of Inquiry into Human Fertilisation and Embryology (1984), chaired by Lady Mary Warnock and popularly known as the Warnock Report, recommended that the human embryo should be protected, and, because the human embryo has the potential for sensory perception 14 days after fertilisation, it recommended that research on embryos after this stage of development should be made illegal. It also recommended that a statutory licensing authority should be established to regulate both research and treatment.

The HUFEA 1990 adopted many of Warnock's recommendations. Under HUFEA, infertility treatments, including artificial insemination by donor, *in vitro* fertilisation and all research activities using *in vitro* embryos are regulated under its licensing authority (HFEA). HFEA vets all proposals for human embryo research. A research licence can permit the creation of living embryos *in vitro* and their use for specified projects of research. The HFEA must be satisfied that the aims of the research fall within the following categories:

- to promote advances in the treatment of infertility;
- to increase knowledge about the causes of congenital disease;
- to increase knowledge about the causes of miscarriages;
- to develop more effective techniques of contraception; and
- to develop methods for pre-implantation detection of gene or chromosome abnormalities in embryos before implantation.

The Act prohibits certain lines of work including:

- genetic modification;
- replacing in the uterus a fertilised egg which has been experimented on;
- growing a fertilised egg for more than 14 days in *in vitro;*
- replacing a human embryo in a non-human animal;
- replacing a nucleus of a cell of an embryo with a nucleus taken from the cell of another person, another embryo or a subsequent development of an embryo (that is, cloning).

However, an *in vitro,* under 14-day-old fetus, a dead fetus or part of it could potentially be classified as a 'product' in a similar way that body products, such as blood or sperm, are capable of being owned once separated from the body (for example, as with the blood samples in *R v. Welsh* and *R v. Rothery,* 1974). Furthermore, there is no statute making it unlawful to own gametes or abortuses or *ex utero* fetal material (Lee & Morgan, 1991).

Although the commercialisation of gametes and embryos or parts of embryos is very strongly depreciated by the Polkinghorne Report (1989), the European Commission's draft directive (COM(88) 496 final-SYN 159) on the patenting of biotechnological inventions does not preclude human fetal material or human parts, although it does specifically exclude the patenting of human beings. If this directive was to have become Community law, then, under our Patenting Act of 1977, fetal material lawfully made available to licensed researchers could properly come to form part of a patentable product, for example, a genetically engineered genetic screening test (McNally & Wheale, 1995).

## Legal Termination of Pregnancy

Sections 58 and 59 of the 1861 Offences Against the Person Act makes it an offence to procure a miscarriage or to supply the means by which a miscarriage might be carried out. The Infant Life Preservation Act of 1929 made it a criminal offence to kill a viable fetus intentionally. There were no further changes to the statutory law on abortion in England until the 1967 Abortion Act. This Act recognises the primacy of the interests and well-being of the mother over those of her fetus, and provides a lawful defence to an action brought under the 1861 and 1929 acts.

In 1990, the 1967 Abortion Act was amended by Section 37 of the HUFEA. Section 1 (1) (d) enables the pregnant woman to elect for abortion of defective fetuses without time limit. Prior to the 'decoupling' of the Infant Life Preservation Act from the 1967 Abortion Act by Section 37 of the HUFEA, a viable fetus with a severe handicap could not be lawfully aborted under Section 1 (1) (b) of the 1967 Act, except when the life of the mother was threatened. Section 1 (1) (d) appears not only utilitarian in intention, but embodies, as Morgan and Lee (1991) suggest, an underlying (negative) eugenics philosophy.

In English common law, parents may claim for 'wrongful birth'. In *Rance and Another v. Mid-Downs Health Authority* (1991), the claim that but for the doctors' negligence in providing ante-natal screening, Mrs. Rance would have been provided with information upon which she would have chosen to abort the child, failed because by the time an abortion could have been performed the fetus was found to be 'capable' of being born alive' under the Infant Life (Preservation) Act 1929. Brooke J found no impropriety in the health authority refusing, or even failing, to advise her of the availability of an abortion at 26 weeks, as the child was capable of being born alive within the meaning of Section 1 of the 1929 Act. *Rance* upheld the sanctity of life principle and demonstrated that, providing the fetus was believed to be viable, an abortion carried out (at that time) before 28 weeks could be unlawful. Contrary to the judgement in *Rance*, however, in *McKay* (see above) the doctor was held to have a duty to advise a patient of the risks of having a handicapped child, to carry out diagnostic procedures and to inform her that termination would be lawful.

The policy of producing children of sound body and mind is being operationalised by ante-natal identification of abnormal fetuses by means of diagnostic genetic screening and subsequent lawful destruction of the genetically defective gamete or fetus. Since *McKay,* the common law thus embodies a new attitude towards the seriously handicapped fetus which has redefined maternal-doctor subjective responsibility, and reinforced the differentiation between the concept of what is a 'normal' and what is an 'abnormal' child.

More than a century ago J.S. Mill's utilitarian calculations focused on the expected quality of the life of the child. If the quality of its life is, on the basis of rational calculation, likely to be undesirable, then it is in its interests that its birth should be prevented. In advising calculations of rational prudence towards the unborn child, J.S. Mill (1864) expresses his position on the child's rights and our duties in his famous *Essay on Liberty,* as follows:

> To bestow a life which may be either a curse or a blessing, unless the being on whom it bestowed will have at least the ordinary chances of a desirable existence, is a crime against that being.

Should a seriously handicapped child be born nowadays, whether through negligence, ignorance of the condition of the fetus or through parental choice? This question was noted by Balcombe L.J. in *Re J* (1990), a court of appeal case in which the court declared it lawful to withhold treatment to a severely handicapped child in cases where: "it may turn out not to be in the child's interests to reserve his life at all costs", a regime of selective non-treatment may be applied. As Smith (1974) observes, in the course of the care-cure of some babies, it may become clear that additional therapy will cost that baby more than he/she can gain.

Lorber (1975) has articulated those criteria he considers appropriate for the selective non-treatment of neonates. Part of his argument for this selection practice is on social utility grounds, and is deemed to be in the interests of those child patients from whom treatment is withheld. This has been likened to the idea of 'passive euthanasia'. However, euthanasia for the fetus or neonate is always involuntary as there is no possibility that the baby can consent to the procedure (Smith, 1974) and the 'substituted judgement' approach is not rationally available to us as a moral justification except as a constructed 'fiction' when the subject is unborn. Thus, we are drawn to the conclusion that, under the guise of 'best interests', the obligation to protect can override the prohibition of killing.

Mason and McCall Smith (1991, p. 148) suggest that if the 'eugenic clause' 1 (1) (d) of the amended Abortion Act 1967 were acknowledged as having been drafted in the fetal, rather than maternal interests, then the right of the handicapped fetus to abortion is then comparable to the defective neonates' right to refuse treatment. Such an acknowledgement would, of course, strengthen the case for accepting 'wrongful life as cause of action.

The technology used for identifying seriously handicapped fetuses is antenatal screening tests, and it is then for doctors and parents to make the calculations availing themselves of approaches such as quality of adjusted life years (QALYs) or quality of well-being scales (see, for example, Baker & Strosberg, 1992) of whether the child's life would be 'desirable'. QALY formulae rank states of health as more or less worthwhile, and, as Lee (1990) remarks, in the final analysis it permits those with the best chance of a prolonged post-operative life to live, and others to die.


## Conclusions

Human genome research is providing scientific knowledge of the genetic determination of disease and genetic predispositions to disorders, and it is this knowledge, together with that derived from embryo research, which underpins many innovations in modern medicine designed to prevent the inheritance of genetic diseases and disorders. In this study, I have attempted to explore the moral and legal consequences of medical technologies derived from human genome research for the fetus (and the child prior to its birth) by identifying the ethics now embodied in the regulation and control of embryo research and the legal termination of pregnancy under English law.

The controversy surrounding the discourse on the question of when human life is deemed to have gained a moral personality was discussed. I argued that, if we believe that the fetus has its own 'intrinsic' value, then moral agents (for example doctors and parents) could have a (special) moral duty towards it and accord it rights commensurate with that duty. Such an assertion of the sanctity of life principle sharply conflicts with the utilitarian approach towards the fetus. For example, it would be morally impermissible to use it merely instrumentally, for example for research purposes. The moral clash of these two positions is that equal respect for individual rights are incompatible with utilitarian calculations of moral prudence.

When legal personality was explored, ambiguity was identified in the common law relating the status of the fetus, and tensions were identified between the sanctity of life principle and the utilitarian approach to life, as embodied in the common law and the civil law as they apply to the child prior to birth and the severely handicapped neonate. Contradictions between the common law and the civil law, and within the civil law itself, were also highlighted. For example, the CDCLA states that a mother cannot be liable for negligence to her own fetus, thus ruling out pre-natal maternal tortious liability except where injuries are sustained as a result of a motor accident, where, under Section 2 of the CDCLA, provision is made for maternal liability in respect of driving a motor vehicle. This maternal duty of care does not apply, however, if the fetus is already seriously handicapped, as the mother of a handicapped child is exempt from liability under the Act for pre-natal harm caused to the child.

While the common law has ruled out any cause of action by a disabled child for 'wrongful life', as discussed above, Section 1 A (1) of the CDCLA provides the child with (effective) grounds for a 'wrongful life' cause of action in circumstances where he/she has a claim against a gamete donor, including its own father, where the child's disabilities arise from his negligence in providing damaged sperm. The law is clear that but for the negligence in giving sperm, that child would never have been born at all, and it may therefore be argued that the disabled child proving negligence but for which he/she would never have been born at all has a 'wrongful life' action. The civil law is here in marked contrast to the English common law where, as discussed above, 'wrongful life' actions are not recognised.

The Law Commission (1974), responding to the utilitarian approach which underpins Section 1 (1) of the CDCLA states that if a child has a legal right to begin life with a sound mind and body, and this is the effect of the proposed legislation, there is a correlative duty on its parents and others to avoid producing conception where the circumstances are likely to result in the birth of a disabled child.

Consideration of the ethics implied by the medical use of embryos for research purposes has demonstrated the unmistakeably predominantly utilitarian approach embedded in the HUFEA. Under HUFEA, a research licence can permit the creation of living embryos *in vitro* and their use for specified projects of research. We also observed that there is no English statute making it unlawful to own gametes or abortuses or *ex utero* fetal material, and patenting law does not preclude the patenting of human fetal material or human parts.

In an exploration of the ethico-legal underpinnings of the legal termination of pregnancy, I argued that, since *McKay,* the common law then embodies a new attitude towards the seriously handicapped fetus which has redefined maternal-doctor subjective responsibility, and reinforces the differentiation between the concept of what is a 'normal' and what is an 'abnormal' child. The policy of producing children of sound body and mind is being operationalised by ante-natal identification of abnormal fetuses by means of diagnostic genetic screening and subsequent lawful destruction of the genetically defective gametes or fetus. I argued that Section 1(1) (d) of the amended 1967

Abortion Act appears not only utilitarian in intention, but embodies an underlying (negative) eugenics philosophy.

Scientific knowledge emanating from human genome research is supporting a form of utilitarianism, based on 'quality of life' values, which has become embedded in the new 'reproductive' technologies and, their corollary, the new negative eugenic technologies. This study has emphasised the ambiguities and contradictions between English common law, which still embodies the sanctity of life principle, and civil law largely now supported, as we have seen, by utilitarian values, as they pertain to the fetus and the child prior to its birth. I contend that the tensions created by these contradictions and ambiguities in the law are producing a 'reflective disequilibrium', in Rawlsian terms, which could bring medical law into disrepute.

**References**

Baker, R. & Strosberg, M. (1992) Triage and equality: an historical reassessment of utilitarian analyses of triage. *Kennedy Institute of Ethics Journal*, **2**, 103-123.

COM(88) 424 final-SYN 146. *Proposal for a Council Decision Adopting a Specific Research Programme in the Field of Health: Predictive Medicine: Human Genome Analysis (1989-1991)*.

COM(88) 496 final-SYN 159. *European Commission's Proposal for a Council Directive on the Legal Protection of Biotechnological Inventions*.

Committee of Inquiry into Human Fertilisation and Embryology (1984) Report. HMSO, London. *D v. Berkshire CC* (1987) 1 All ER 20.

Glover, J. (1990) *Causing Death and Saving Lives*. Penguin, London, 124-125.

Griffin, J. (1992) *Well Being*. London, Clarendon Paperbacks, Parts I and II.

Grobstein, C. (1981) *From Chance to Purpose* Addison-Wesley, London.

Hare, R.M. (1988) When does potentiality count? A comment on Lockwood. *Bioethics*, **2**, 214-226.

Harris, J. (1985) *The Value of Life*. Routledge, London, 11.

Kant, I. (1948) *Groundwork of the Metaphysic of Morals*. Translated by Paton H.J. and published as *The Moral Law*. Hutchinson.

Kennedy, I. (1988) *Treat Me Right: Essays in Medical Law and Ethics*. Clarendon Press, Oxford.

Law Commission (1974) *Injuries on Unborn Children*. Report no. 60.

Lee, R. (1990) To be or not to be: is that the question? The claim of wrongful life. In Lee, R. & Morgan, D. (eds) (1991) *Birthrights: Law at the Beginnings of Life*. Routledge, London.

Lorber, J. (1975) Ethical problems in the management of myelomeningocele and hydrocephalus. *Journal of the Royal College of Physicians*, **10**, 47-59.

Macfarlane, L.J. (1990) *The Theory and Practice of Human Rights.*Cambridge University Press, Cambridge.

Mason, J.K. & McCall Smith, R.A. (1991) *Law and Medical Ethics.* Butterworths, London, 148.

*McKay v Essex Area Health Authority* [1982] 2 All ER 771.

McNally, R. & Wheale, P.R. (1995) Bio-patenting and innovation: a new industrial divide? In Morrisey, D. (ed.) *Biotechnological Innovation, Societal Responses and Policy Implications, pp.* 7-17.

Mill, J.S. *(1864)* Essay on Liberty, 3rd edn. In Warnock, M. (ed.) *Utilitarianism.* Fotana, London.

Morgan, D. & Lee, R. (eds) (1991) *Human Fertilisation and Embryology Act 1990.* Blackstone Press, 48.

*Paton v. Trustees of British Pregnancy Advisory Service* (1989) 2 All ER 987 (1989) QB 287.

Polkingthorne Report (1989) *Review of the Guidance on the Research Using of Fetuses and Fetal Material.* HMSO, London.

*Rance and Another v. Mid-Downs Health Authority* [1991] 1 All ER 801.

Rawls, J. (1972) *A Theory of Justice.* Oxford University Press, Oxford.

*Re F (in utero)* (1988) Fam 122 [1988] 2 All ER 193.

*Re J* (a minor) (1990) 3 All ER 930, CA. at 942.

*Report on Injuries to Unborn Children* (1974) Report no. 60, cmnd 5709. HSMO, London, para. 59.

*Re S* (Adult: Refusal of Treatment) Fam (1992).

*R v. Tait* (1989) *The Times,* 26 April, CA.

*R v. Welsh [1974]* RTR 478, CA and *R v. Rothery* [1976] RTR 550, CA.

Smith, D.H. (1974) On letting some babies die. *Hastings Centre Studies,* **2**, 93-101.

STOA (1992) *Bioethics in Europe.* European Parliament, Luxembourg.

Strong, C. (1991) Delivering hydrocephalic fetuses. *Bioethics,* **5**, 1-22.

Tooley, M. (1972) Abortion and infanticide. *Philosophy and Public Affairs,* **2**, 37-65.

Whitefield, A. (1993) Common law duties to unborn children. *Medical Law Review,* **1**, 28-52.

# 8 The American Gene Therapy Industry and the Social Shaping of a New Technology

PAUL MARTIN

ABSTRACT        *This chapter examines the commercial development of gene therapy and describes the creation of the American gene therapy industry and the different ways in which firms are developing the technology as both a clinical tool and a commodity. In particular, it focuses on the industry debate over how gene therapy can be used in clinical practice and how firms can make money out of this. A number of different conceptions for the application of gene therapy are described and related to the choices being made by firms for the design of the technology itself. Some reflections on the way in which gene therapy has been shaped in the process of commercialisation will be made.*

## Introduction

This chapter describes one part of a larger project which is attempting to write a historical sociology of the early development of an important new medical technology - gene therapy. It draws upon concepts from both social theory and empirical studies in evolutionary economics. In particular, the chapter focuses on the process by which a set of scientific ideas and techniques is transformed into both a working technology and a commodity.

Gene therapy promises to one of the most important technologies to benefit from the Human Genome Mapping Project (HGMP). It can be defined simply as "the delivery of functional genes to somatic tissue for the treatment of disease", and is a radically new approach to therapeutics. Gene therapy is already being developed for a wide range of genetic and acquired diseases, including cancer, human immunodeficiency virus (HIV)/AIDS and arthritis. The reference to somatic tissues distinguishes it from germline gene therapy, which would pass changes on to future generations. This is not being developed at present because of the profound ethical issues it raises.

97

The idea of gene therapy is almost as old as that of molecular biology itself, and itself, and predates the HGMP by almost three decades.  One of the first suggestions of using genes for the treatment of disease was made by Tatum in his Nobel Prize acceptance speech in 1958.  Then, in 1962, Szybalski coined the term 'gene therapy', following his successful attempt at mammalian gene transfer.  However, it took until 1990 before the first ever human clinical trial for gene therapy commenced in the US.

Since the 1990 trial, some 98 other clinical trials have been approved in the US (as of December 1994).  One striking feature of these trials is that the great majority (71) are aimed at the treatment of cancer, with only 14 targeting a genetic disease and a further seven aimed at HIV/AIDS.  It is now the case that many scientists and clinicians working on gene therapy see it as a general therapeutic modality which can be applied to almost any disease, regardless of its cause.

America has also led the way in looking to exploit gene therapy commercially.  Some 20 dedicated gene therapy firms have been founded to develop gene therapy products and services, with a combined valuation of over $1 billion.  This is despite the fact that no gene therapy product will be on the market until at least the end of the decade, and no patient can be said to have clearly benefited from the use of gene therapy to date.

## The Science of Gene Therapy

To simplify, human gene transfer systems used in gene therapy are composed of three distinct elements:

(1)     the therapeutic gene - containing the information required to make the therapeutic protein;

(2)     an expression system - this consists of DNA sequences which flank the therapeutic gene, and control when and in what tissues or cells it can be 'turned on ';

(3)     a delivery system or vector - to allow the gene to enter the body, avoid degradation and be targeted to the desired site in the body (cell type).  The expression system must be contained in a delivery system (or vector).

The main commercial focus of all gene therapy companies in the development of gene delivery systems which can be used in a particular clinical application, as most firms intend to license genes and expression systems from third parties.

Delivery systems can be divided into two groups, viral vectors and non-viral delivery systems.

## Viral Vectors

Vectors composed of modified viruses have the advantage of being biologically specific, i.e. they only infect particular cell types, are able to easily enter and be expressed in cells, and can be manipulated to carry a therapeutic 'payload'. However, there are a number of safety concerns associated with the use of these potentially infectious agents. The main types of viral vectors used are based on retroviruses and adenoviruses.

## Non-viral Delivery Systems

Non-viral delivery systems have been more difficult to design and are still in their early stages of development. They are not biologically specific to a given cell type and do not enter cells in the body as readily as viral vectors. In this sense, they have to be guided physically or biologically to the target site. However, they have none of the safety problems associated with viral vectors. The three main types of non-viral delivery systems are liposomes, direct injection and electroporation (Table 1).

**Table 1.** Characteristics of the main delivery systems

| Vector | Target cell type | Length of expression | Cell targeting *in vivo* | Safety |
|---|---|---|---|---|
| Retroviral | Dividing only | Long | Yes | Possibly carcinogenic |
| Adenoviral | All | Short | Yes | Causes inflammation |
| Liposome | All | Medium | Require guiding molecules | Safe |
| Naked DNA | Muscle | Medium | No | Safe |
| Electroporation | All-only in culture | Long | Not applicable | Safe |

There are two discrete ways in which these delivery system are being applied;

(1)  *Ex vivo* gene therapy, where the modification of the patient's cells occurs outside the body. In *ex vivo* therapies, cells are removed from the body, genetically altered the culture and returned to the patient, for example by blood transfusion or bone marrow transplantation.

(2)    *In vivo* gene therapy, where the genetic alteration of the cells occurs by direct administration of the therapy to the patient. *In vivo* therapies are mainly administered by injection or in an aerosol spray to the lungs.

For technical reasons, the use of retroviral vectors and electroporation is mainly restricted to *ex vivo* approaches. In contrast, adenoviral vectors, liposomes and naked DNA can be used in either *ex vivo* or *in vivo* approaches, but are predominantly used *in vivo*.

## Commercialisation of Gene Therapy in the US

Some 30 business firms have been founded in the last 8 years to commercialise gene therapy in the US, and include both dedicated gene therapy firms and dedicated cell therapy companies. The latter are primarily concerned with developing cell-based therapies (cell replacement and engineering), but many of these are also looking to produce gene therapies. In addition, a further 20-25 biotechnology companies have established gene therapy research programmes, while some 15-20 firms have been founded to work on the closely related area of oligonucleotide and antisense technology. The major firms in each of these areas and the dates they were founded are shown in Table 2.

One of the striking features of the commercial development of gene therapy is that very few of the large 'first tier' biotechnology companies, and none of the major pharmaceutical companies in the US, were involved in developing gene therapy until about 1993. One of the large biopharmaceutical companies, such as Amgen, Genentech and Biogen, only a handful have founded subsidiaries or set up in-house research programmes in this area. Furthermore, few of the large multinational pharmaceutical companies have made investments in the dedicated gene therapy firms, and most have only just started to form collaborations with them.

It is therefore clear that neither the scientific nor commercial development of gene therapy has occurred in existing producers of therapeutics, but has required the creation of a series of new firms to drive this process. This is perhaps explained by the fact that gene therapy operates within a radically different conceptual 'paradigm' from traditional pharmaceuticals.

A summary of the gene therapies being developed by ten of the leading dedicated firms is shown in Table 3. At present, none of these companies has any product on the market, and it will be several years before one is launched.

A number of key points emerge from Table 3. In particular, it is clear that a wide range of different vector technologies, disease targets and clinical applications are being worked on by different firms. There is no one dominant 'design' for gene delivery technology at present, although the use of retroviral vectors is common and both genetic and acquired diseases are being targeted.

## Evolution of Firm Strategies

Like many other areas of biotechnology, almost all the dedicated gene therapy firms were founded by leading academic researchers, many of whom were instrumental in developing gene transfer techniques. The firms were initially set up with the help of entrepreneurs and venture capitalists, often as a way of commercialising the techniques being developed by scientists in a particular research institution. It is interesting to note that the first wave of firms was founded in 1987-1988, several years before the first clinical trial of the therapy was approved, and at a time when many technical problems were yet to be overcome.

The founders used two key assets in order to raise the institutional support and initial venture funds needed to establish these companies. The first was their credibility, skill and 'know-how' and the second was the patents they held on core technologies. As a consequence, any given firm inherited a given set of proprietary techniques and the specific research agenda developed by the founding scientists, both of which it was committed to from its inception. In this sense, gene therapy firms were initially established as little more than private research organisations, and were, to some extent, 'locked into' the development of a particular vector technology by the intellectual property they held.

As these firms have developed, they have had to raise additional funds, often by flotation on the stock market, and form partnerships with other, larger, companies possessing the substantial resources and complementary assets required to take potential therapies through clinical trials. This has required the gene therapy firms to develop a much greater 'commercial focus' and a clear business strategy, paying special attention to strengthening their management, justifying their choice of delivery technology and anticipating the types of products and services they will sell in the future.

One of the first signs of these changes has been the recruitment of specialists management. While the founder scientists have remained centrally involved in the running of nearly all these companies, normally as directors of research, board directors or consultants, most firms have recruited senior executives from the biopharmaceutical and pharmaceutical industry to act as either

**Table 2.** Main companies working on gene therapy and related technologies in the US (with date of foundation)

| Dedicated gene therapy firms | Other biotechnology firms working on gene therapy |
|---|---|
| Public | |
| GeneMedicine (1992) | Agracetus (1981) |
| Genetic Therapy (1987) | Alkermes (1987) |
| Somatix Therapy (1988) | Alpha Therapeutic (1947) |
| Targeted Genetics (1989) | Anticancer (1984) |
| TransKaryotic Therapies (1988) | Apollon (1992) |
| Viagene (1987) | Aviron (1992) |
| Vical (1987) | Centocor (1979) |
| | Chiron (1980) |
| Private | CV Therapeutics (1992) |
| Avigen | Cytocare (1984) |
| Canji (1990) | Cytrx (1985) |
| Genetix Pharmaceuticals (1992) | Genetics Institute (1980) |
| Genovo (1994) | Gliatech (1988) |
| GenVec (1993) | Immunicon (1984) |
| Introgen (1993) | Inex (1992) |
| Megabios (1992) | Medicorp (1985) |
| Rgene Therapeutics (1994) | OncorPharm (1991) |
| | Pharmagenics (1990) |
| Spin-offs/subsidiaries | Repligen (1981) |
| Ariad Gene Therapeutics (1994) | Therion Biologics (1991) |
| Genetronics (BTX) (1983) | |
| Ingenex (Titan Pharma) | |
| Neozyme II (Genzyme) (1990) | |
| TargeTech (Immune Response) (1989) | |

| Cell therapy firms | Anti-sense and oligonucleotide firms |
|---|---|
| Aastrom Biosciences (1989) | Antivirals (1981) |
| ACT Biomedical (1985) | Athena Neuroscience (1986) |
| Alexion Pharmaceuticals (1992) | Genelabs (1984) |
| Applied Immune Sciences (1985) | Genetic MediSyn |
| Cell Genesys (1988) | Genta (1988) |
| CellPro (1987) | Gilead Sciences (1987) |
| Cytotherapeutics (1989) | Hybridon (1989) |
| Genzyme Tissue Repair (1987) | Isis Pharmaceuticals |
| Systemix (1988) | Lynx Pharmaceuticals |
| Progenitor (Interneuron) | NeoRx (1984) |
| | Ribozyme Pharmaceuticals (1992) |
| | Texas Biotechnology (1991) |
| | Triplex (1989) |

## Table 3. Leading dedicated gene therapy companies in the US

| Name | Founded | Vector technology | Disease targets | Clinical use | Product | Mk.cap | No of staff |
|---|---|---|---|---|---|---|---|
| Avigen | 1992 | Adeno-associated virus | Sickle cell, thallasseamia, viral infection, chemotherapy | Injectables (outpatients) | Gene drugs | Private | 30 |
| GeneMedicine | 1992 | Lipid/DNA complex | Haemophilia, muscle wasting, vascular disease, RA | Injectables (outpatients) | Gene drugs | NA | 70 |
| Genetic Therapy, Inc. | 1987 | Retrovirus, adenvirus | Brain, breast and lung cancer, Gaucher's, CF | *Ex vivo therapy* and adjuncts to surgery (inpatients) | Vetors/cells for surgery and gene transplants | US$211 million | 90 |
| GenVec | 1993 | Adeno-associated virus, adenovirus, liposomes | CF, lung cancer, Gaucher's RA, Parkinson's/Alzheimer's | Aerosol (outpatients) ex vivo therapy (inpatients) vectors/cells | Gene drugs and vectors/cells for gene transplants | Private | NA |
| Somatix | 1988 | Retrovirus/adenovirus, adeno-associated virus | Renal, breast and skin cancer, Parkinson's haemophilia | *Ex vivo* therapy (inpatients) | Vetors/cells for gene transplants | US$117 million | 80 |
| TargeTech | 1989 | Ligand/DNA complex | Hepititis B, Haemophilia, liver diseases | Injectables (outpatients) | Gene drugs | Private | NA |
| Targeted Genetics | 1989 | Retrovirus, adeno-associated virus | HIV, CF | *Ex vivo* therapy (inpatients), aerosol (outpatients) | Gene transplant services gene drugs | NA | 50 |
| TransKaryotic Therapies | 1988 | Electroporation | Renal cancer, haemophilia, growth hormone deficiency | Injectables (outpatients) | Cell-based drugs | NA | 60 |
| Viagene | 1987 | Retrovirus | HIV and other viral infections, skin and cervical cancer | Vaccines (outpatients), ex vivo, therapy (inpatients) | Vaccines and vectors/cells for gene transplants | US$101 million | 120 |
| Vical | 1987 | Naked DNA, liposomes | Viral infections, heart disease, cancer, haemophilia | Vaccines (outpatients) injectables (outpatients) ex vivo therapy (inpatients | Vaccines, gene drugsand vectors/ cells for gene transplants | US$154 | 60 |

CF = cystic Fibrosis; RA = Rheumatoid arthritis; Mk.cap = stock market value of company (NASDAQ), March 1994; NA = Information not available chief executive officers or business managers. Furthermore, as the firms have started to move towards clinical trials, other managers with experience of project management, regulatory affairs and large-scale production have been recruited to execute the expanding range of functions within the firm.

However, the shift towards a 'commercial focus' is most clearly visible in what might be called the firm's technology strategy. It is set out in the documents produced to raise institutional support, and, in particular, for the firm's initial public offering to the stock exchange. The technology strategy focuses heavily on the anticipated clinical applications of the company's gene therapy and the types of produce or service which the firm intends to sell.

At present, no gene therapy has been demonstrated to be clinically effective and no produce or service is commercially available. It is therefore difficult to talk about a 'market' for gene therapy products, or even to be certain about how they will be used in clinical practice, as no one is able to predict which technologies can be demonstrated to be safe, efficacious and cost-effective in clinical trials. In this sense, firms are developing their technologies in conditions of ignorance about both their technical clinical and commercial chances of success.

A firm therefore has to construct its strategy for the development of its gene delivery system on the basis of:

- the techniques they 'own' through patents;
- assumptions about how these techniques might be used in clinical practice;
- ideas of how they could be sold as a product or service.

In particular, firms appear to be drawing heavily on experience from the use and commercialisation of other related medical technologies in order to 'visualise' how their gene therapy might be used and sold in the future.

Once the strategy has been chosen, the firm then uses it to guide decisions about investing in the development of particular gene delivery systems and the design of clinical trials. The trial is important, as it can be seen a both an attempt to establish the technical performance of the technology and to see if it is possible to incorporate the new practices associated with gene therapy into the clinic.

Despite the diversity of delivery techniques shown in Table 3, two main divisions between firms can be distinguished with respect to their technology strategies. The first is the choice between using either viral or non-viral vectors. The second is the choice of the product (or service) to sell; this, in turn, is closely related to the firm's decision to invest in either *ex vivo* or *in vivo* therapy.

These choices are the central debates among business managers in the gene therapy industry, and are heavily contested in public. The debate about vectors is mainly concerned with safety risks, while the debate about products focuses on business strategy and how firms can make money out of gene therapy. However, they both ultimately revolve around different and competing conceptions of how gene therapy will be used by doctors. Given the lack of hard information about the safety of different vectors in human trials and the fact that many gene therapies have almost no medical precedent, these arguments are essentially rhetorical at present.

## Visualising Gene Therapy: Constructing Clinical Uses and Markets

Three distinct conceptions of how gene therapy might be clinically used and commercialised can be seen in the strategies of the gene therapy firms mentioned in Table 3.

### Gene Transplants (Ex Vivo Gene Therapy)

The first attempts at the clinical application of gene therapy were what might be called gene transplants. Here, the goal is to 'transplant' a gene into a group of the patient's cells so that they can either correct a genetic defect by making a missing protein or produce a new protein which may help to combat an acquired disease. The development of this approach dominated the first clinical trials of gene therapy in the 1990s, and it is still being used in a majority of the current round of trials. Most protocols have used retroviral vectors (Table 4).

**Table 4.** *Ex vivo* gene therapy steps

| | |
|---|---|
| (1) | Remove cells from a patient's bone marrow, blood or liver |
| (2) | Culture the cells in a laboratory |
| (3) | Transfer the therapeutic gene into the dividing cells using a (retroviral) vector |
| (4) | Grow large numbers of the genetically modified cells *in vitro* |
| (5) | Re-implant the cells back into the patient |

*Ex vivo* gene therapy has been unsuccessfully carried out in animal models, and is the only gene therapy strategy to have demonstrated a therapeutic benefit in human clinical trials with the treatment of rare human genetic diseases, such as severe familial hyper-cholesterolaemia. It is essentially a surgical procedure requiring inpatient admission, and is very similar to the established practice of autologous bone marrow transplantation. Treatment is unique to each patient, and is therefore costly.

Firms are adopting two types of commercial strategy to develop gene transplants (*ex vivo* gene therapy). A number of dedicated gene therapy firms (e.g. Targeted Genetics) and several cell therapy firms are establishing their own 'cell service centres' or 'cell farms' in order to sell the culturing and genetic modification of patients' cells. This strategy looks to extend the existing market for commercial services associated with bone marrow transplantation, which is already worth several hundred million dollars. Other companies (e.g. GTI) are simply aiming to act as third party suppliers of retroviral vectors and cell lines for *ex vivo* procedures, rather than become direct service providers themselves.

Advocates of *ex vivo* gene therapy see a number of benefits of this approach, including the fact that it has been shown to work, is now relatively established, involves modifying cells in controlled conditions and is closely related to existing procedures (blood transfusion/bone marrow transplantation). In justifying its pursuit of *ex vivo* approach Somatix states:

> The company believes that its *ex vivo* approach has the potential to be commercialised more quickly than the alternative *in vivo* approach, ... The advantages of the *ex vivo* approach include greater control over the number and type of cells that are genetically modified and the amount of protein produced. In addition, the *ex vivo* approach may facilitate pre-clinical and clinical development because studies can be more easily designed and results more readily measured (Somatix Therapy Corporation, 1992).

However, there are now many firms who regard *ex vivo* approaches in general, and the use of retroviral vectors in particular, as highly problematic. As Avigen notes, there are major safety worries and significant technical limitations associated with the use of retroviral vectors (Avigen, Inc., 1993).

Other firms reject all *ex vivo* approaches on largely commercial grounds. This is because they involve difficult cell culturing which has to be performed to a very high standard to avoid infection, and are therefore both risky and labour-intensive. As GeneMedicine argues:

> The company believes that these *ex vivo* and viral-based gene therapy approaches have significant therapeutic limitations ... The *ex vivo* approach involves a cumbersome and expensive process, which may reduce physician and patient acceptance and limit its use to serious diseases without alternative therapies (Gene Medicine, Inc. , 1994).

In response to these safety worries and the potentially high cost of therapy, some firms working on retroviral mediated *ex vivo* therapy (e.g. genetic therapy) are increasingly focusing their commercial strategy on the treatment of life-threatening diseases, such as cancer, where safety and cost are less of a concern. Other firms (Somatix) are looking to move away from the use of retroviral vectors altogether.

## Gene Drugs *(*In Vivo *Gene Therapy)*

For many firms in the gene therapy industry, the commercial 'holy grail' is the development of therapies which can be sold as conventional pharmaceutical products, or 'genes in a bottle'. These would be based on the direct genetic modification of a patient's cells in the body (*in vivo*), using either viral or non-viral vectors (Table 5). In many ways, this approach is similar to the established use of injectable or orally administered hormones, such as oestrogen, which directly alter gene expression in many cells.

A number of clinical trials are already under way to test *in vivo* approaches for the treatment of cystic fibrosis where the gene is administered to the lung in an aerosol spray. These follow positive results in animal models. Other trials, using the direct injection of DNA or liposomes, started in 1995.

**Table 5.** *In vivo* gene therapy steps

| | |
|---|---|
| (1) | Diagnosis |
| (2) | Treatment at outpatient or general practitioner clinics by the simple administration (normally injection) or a standardised therapeutic which would be used on all patients with the same condition |

The firms developing gene drugs are aiming to create therapies which are very similar to conventional medicines. They are being designed to be administered in a outpatient setting, are easily stored and have a limited life in the body. This would make them easy to use, reduce their costs and increase their availability. Some firms (e.g. Avigen, GeneMedicine and TargeTech) are seeking to develop 'platform technologies' which can be used to deliver a range of therapeutic proteins systemically for the treatment of a variety of chronic diseases.

*In vivo* approaches are still in their early stages, however. For their advocates, they offer many therapeutic and commercial advantages over *ex vivo* approaches. GeneMedicine is developing non-viral vectors for *in vivo* application, and justifies this by arguing:

> The company believes that its gene medicines will have significant clinical advantages over other gene therapy methods, which include the use of viruses and cell transplantation. The potential advantages ... include (i) direction administration to patients by conventional methods, (ii) their ability to degrade from the body by natural processes, and (iii) the ability of the physician to administer the gene medicine repeatedly, allowing modification of the treatment regimen ... (GeneMedicine, Inc., 1994).

The firm also notes that there are many commercial attractions of developing genes as drugs, as they will be branded products which can be sold through existing distribution chains (drug companies) and will require repeated administration in contrast to other, one-off gene therapies.

Despite these clear commercial advantages, some firms remain sceptical about *in vivo* technology on both technical and clinical grounds. The principle of an easily administered gene therapy which can be selectively taken up by the target cells after injection into the bloodstream has yet to be convincingly demonstrated. Furthermore:

> Many *in vivo* systems have limited dosing precision. For example, some systems result in the incorporation of the desired genes into different parts of the genome in individual cells, leading to a wide variation in, and unpredictability, of, protein expression (TransKaryoticTherapies, Inc., 1993).

In response to these criticisms, several firms (GeneMedicine, Avigen) are developing expression systems which can be controlled by orally administered compounds and would allow doctors to modulate the therapy easily. Targeting is also being improved by either administering the injectable drug directly to specific tissue types (e.g. bone marrow) or binding a lipid delivery system to a cell-specific ligand.

*Bespoke Drug Delivery*

In contrast to almost all other approaches being attempted, one firm, TransKaryotic Therapies (TKT), is developing *ex vivo* gene therapy for application by direct subcutaneous injection (Table 6). This approach sees gene therapy as 'an *in vivo* protein production and delivery system', and seeks to develop what are, in effect, drugs tailor-made for each patient. It is a genuinely novel strategy almost without medical precedent.

This form of gene therapy has only just gone into its first clinical trial, but the overall strategy has been successfully demonstrated in animal models.

**Table 6.** Bespoke drug delivery steps

| | |
|---|---|
| (1) | Remove a very small patch of skin from the patient in an outpatient setting using a punch biopsy |
| (2) | Pack the skin sample on ice and send it to the company's central processing laboratories where skin cells are isolated and grown in culture |
| (3) | Insert the therapeutic gene into the skin cell's chromosomes using a non-viral technique (electroporation) |
| (4) | Isolate and characterise a single cell expressing the required gene, then grow this single cell in bulk |
| (5) | Pack the cells into a syringe and send this back to the clinic on ice |
| (6) | Give the patient an injection of their own modified cells just under the skin |

TKT claims that this approach would have a number of important advantages over both existing *ex vivo* and *in vivo* approaches. In particular, the cells used can be well characterised, the genetic changes will be minimal, the expression of the protein can be predictable and, as a consequence, the system as a whole will be safe. Furthermore:

> This patient-specific protein production and delivery system has a number of additional clinical and commercial advantages as compared to intermittent protein injections. Most importantly, TKT's gene therapy system represents an actual cure-one gene therapy treatment has the potential to last a patient's lifetime (TransKaryotc Therapies, Inc., 1992).

Its strategy for commercialisation involves developing the injection of modified skin cells as a platform technology for the systemic delivery of already well-understood protein drugs, such as human growth hormone, insulin and erythropoietic. The firm would operate a number of centralised processing units where all cells would be handled.

*Summary*

Three competing conceptions for the clinical use and commercialisation of gene therapy have been identified. To some extent, these different conceptions of use relate to the choices mentioned earlier between viral and non-viral vectors, and between *ex vivo* or *in vivo* approaches. A matrix of these choices is shown in Figure 1, where the major firms and the different conceptions of use for gene therapy are mapped out.

Most firms are committed to developing only one type of product, but a number (Somatix, Genetic Therapy, Targeted Genetics and GenVec) are working on both gene transplants and gene drugs. However, at the end of 1994, only one company, GenVec was developing both viral and non-viral delivery systems.

## Gene Therapy: From Science to Technology

*The Actors in the Innovation Process and the Problematisation of Development*

When the first firms were established in 1987, gene therapy was still essentially a scientific research topic. At the time, the principle of using genes to help fight disease had only recently been demonstrated in animal models, and there were still many technical and regulatory problems to be overcome before it could even be tested on human subjects. Until this point, the only actors involved in the development of gene therapy had been scientists working on particular gene transfer techniques and the treatment of rare genetic diseases. Surprisingly, this did not prevent half a dozen firms from being established as essentially private research organisations with the aim of commercialising the work of these leading scientists.

By the early 1990s, with the growth of clinical trials, clinicians became involved in the innovation process and started to apply gene therapy to a wide range of clinical problems. As a consequence, the research agenda appears to have shifted, with the emphasis increasingly on the development of gene therapy as a general therapeutic modality being applied to a number of acquired diseases, in particular cancer.

At around the same time as the first clinical trials, dedicated firms started to pay increasing attention to how gene therapy might be used routinely in the clinic and how they could make money out of it. This appears to be partly a consequence of the changing focus of firms as they recruited managers from the pharmaceutical industry, but was also forced on them as they tried to raise additional funds from the capital markets. With the creation of gene therapy firms, a new set of actors entered the innovation process, with both the capacity to carry out research and a clear aim to develop it in such far greater resources at their disposal and can perform a number of different functions simultaneously. The firm is therefore able to act as one of the key sites in the innovation process, as it can integrate technical, regulatory and commercial considerations and use these to direct its research and development programme.

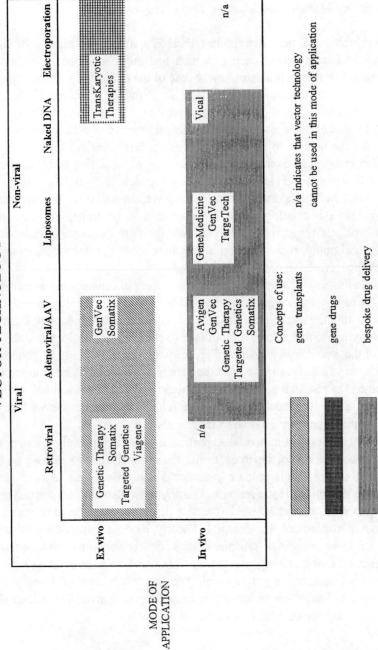

**Figure 1.** Summary of firm technology choices

## Constructing Markets and Shaping Technologies

The development of gene therapy has, therefore, involved a number of different actors at different times, each of which has thought about gene therapy in relationship to different problems. In the case of the dedicated gene therapy firms, they have 'problematised' gene therapy in terms of its clinical use and its commodity form. In particular, one key question has been posed: 'how can gene therapy be successfully integrated into clinical practice in such a way as to make money for the firm?'. In attempting to answer this question, firms have had to decide between trying to incorporate gene therapy into existing patterns of clinical work and trying to create completely new practices. In the case of 'gene transplants' and 'gene drugs', some firms have chosen to try to integrate gene therapy into the existing markets for bone marrow transplant services and pharmaceuticals respectively. In contrast, the firm developing 'bespoke drug delivery' is hoping to create a completely new set of clinical practices and, as a consequence, create an entirely new market.

In this sense, firms are engaged in a process of constructing markets at the same time as they are designing the new technology. Thus, the way in which firms are anticipating the use of gene therapy is fundamental to the development of the technology itself, and affects both the firm's choice of technology and the actual design of the gene delivery system. For example, the attempts to fit gene therapy into a pharmaceutical paradigm, with the design of 'gene drugs', has fundamentally determined the research agenda for the development of these technologies. This is clearly seen with GeneMedicine's research to create liposome vectors which behave just like conventional pharmacenticals.

All moves to commercialise particular gene therapies therefore critically depend on convincing doctors to use them. The clinical trial is a major part of this process as it provides legitimate 'evidence' about efficacy and advantages over alternative therapies. However, gene therapy must also be incorporated into the existing system of medical work (practices), and his is going to be easier if the changes required are only incremental. Clearly, by conceiving of gene therapy in terms of bone marrow transplantations or conventional pharmaceuticals, companies are trying to bring gene therapy into use within the existing regimen of progressional work, training and control. The alternative route of developing gene therapy as a radically new practice (i.e. bespoke gene delivery) runs the risk of it not being easily incorporated into medical work.

## Conclusion

With the entry of the firm into the innovation process, increasing attention has been given to the development of gene therapy as a commodity. Central to this process have been attempts to visualise how gene therapy might be used in medical practice, and firms have developed different models of its potential application and commercialisation.

The choice of a particular model for the product is heavily influenced by the technology available to a firm, but also reflects a judgement about the clinical and commercial benefits of pursuing a particular route. This is a social and economic judgement which fundamentally shapes both the technology developed by the firm and the exact design of the technical artefact itself. At each stage of the career of gene therapy, there has been a dynamic interaction between attempts to 'visualise' how gene therapy might be used, a programme of research based on a particular set of problems associated with this conception, and attempts to test prototypes of the concept in experimental systems. Throughout this process the technology itself has been shaped and reshaped, and has, in effect, co-evolved with the changing ideas of its application.

## References

Avigen, Inc. (1993) *Avigen: Corporate profile.* Avigen Inc., Alameda, CAN, USA.

GeneMedicine, Inc. (1994) *Common Stock Offer Document.* Issued July 1994 by GeneMedicine, Inc., Houston, TX, USA.

TransKaryotic Therapies, Inc. (1992) *TKT's Gene Therapy Program.* TransKaryotic Therapies Inc., Cambridge, MA, USA.

TransKaryoic Therapies, Inc. (1993) *Common Stock Offer Document.* Issued July 1993 by TransKaryotic Therapies, Inc., Cambridge, MA, USA.

# 9 Social Criticism and the Human Genome Programme: Some Reflections on the Limits of a Limited Social Science

HILARY ROSE

ABSTRACT    *The question of how far the risk of a new eugenicism is sufficiently different from the old is explored from the perspectives of different actors in the social shaping of the new genetics. US and UK critical voices are contrasted, together with that of an international opposition feminist grouping. The paper suggests that it is timely for science, technology and society researchers to move beyond their rich but mostly non-formative analyses, towards actively helping to expand the networks, and through this the possibility of a democratic and normatively reshaped technoscience.*

## Introduction

Close to the fiftieth celebration of Victory in Europe (VE) day, there is still not peace in Europe. Instead, there is ethnic cleansing, a recrudescent neo-Nazim in our midst and a political response on the part of other European powers remarkably reminiscent of appeasement. When considering the human genome project (HGP), I find myself increasingly uncomfortable at the ease with which the risk of a new eugenicism, sustained by the new genetics, has been dismissed.

On one level I agree with Evelyn Fox Keller that: "It is true, of course, that in 1990 we have no Nazi conspiracy to fear. All we have to fear today is our own complacency that there are some right hands in which to invest this responsibility - above all, the responsibility for arbitrating normality" (Keller, 1992, p. 299). However, on another I find myself uneasy as to whether a new eugenicism is sufficiently different from the old. Certainly, there are more than traces of eugenics scattered around the HGP literature. Although it is written without the language of hatred for an *untermenschen,* there is a eugenicism that is taken for granted embedded within medical technology - the increasing array of diagnostic tests. Bertrand Jordan accurately reflects: "The impact of the genome programme on society as a whole is far from insignificant. The new knowledge thus gained leads to the elimination of embryos through prenatal diagnosis and pregnancy termination" (Jordan, 1993, p. 168).

Although personal choice about keeping or not keeping a particular pregnancy is stressed within the literature of clinical genetics, the profession in the UK consistently makes clear to the state the economic benefits to be gained if the numbers of seriously genetically impaired infants go down. Pointing to the statistic that genetic impairment only constitutes 3% of all impairment may weaken the cost-benefit effectiveness of such a claim. However, it does not tackle the taken for granted eugenicism in which some right hands decide which of the impaired fetuses need to have maternal decisions made about their survival (Hubbard, 1984). Nor does testing which claims to give reassurance actually provide it (Green, 1990). Scarcely surprisingly, the movement of disabled people is deeply suspicious about the proliferation of genetic testing (Shakespeare, 1995).

Thus, the question of sufficient difference nags away beneath this chapter's discussion of the social criticism of the HGP. Who are the actors, and what are their alliances within both the natural and the social sciences and with the new social movements? Neither the HGP nor its critics are identical cross-nationally, so how are there differences to be understood? In addition, do the critics seek to block science as many leading geneticists claim, or do they seek to shape science in new directions?

## Origin Stories

The HGP has two distinctly whiggish and linked histories as told by scientists and science writers. First, there is an internalist account, which begins with a number of precursor research findings and culminates in 1953, with Crick and Watson's helical model of DNA which is seen as the crucial 'launch pad' for the new genetics. Then, there is an externalist history, which locates the launching of this immense international effort to map and sequence the human genome at a meeting of most of the insignificant figures in the field, convened by Robert Sinsheimes in Santa Cruz in May 1985. Unlike this carefully orchestrated political/technical bid, which energetically corresponds with the actor network analyses of social science accounts (Callon, 1987), the UK version celebrates the casual word in the right ear beloved of UK elite political storytelling (Bodmer & McKie, 1994).

However, the story as told by leading actors (and one of the interesting things about science is how frequently its practitioners not only want to construct the knowledge but also the history of the knowledge) is that the HGP was, from its inception, a highly self-conscious bringing together of different scientific, industrial and political interests. In each country, these networks reflect different configurations of interest. For example, while the French complained about the lack of industrial interest in making laboratory equipment, they rejoiced in national technophilia, and so experienced very little opposition (Jordan, 1993). In contrast, the key US actors were well aware of potential controversy, and planned for 5% of the budget to be dedicated to the ethical, legal and social implications (ELSI) of the HGP. With more confidence than the British were to display, the US placed a philosopher (Eric Juengst at the National Institutes of Health, NIH) and a jurist (Michael Yesley at the Department of the Environment) in joint charge.

In addition, global networks needed to be constructed, moving from the standard form of open international scientific unions, which agree standards and measures, to the establishment of a new international scientific organisation, the Human Genome Organisation (HUGO), which actually selects its members. Such networks had to be made sufficiently stable so as to constitute and reflect stable knowledge and technological know-how. In the early years, the self-appointed HUGO played a crucial part in this networking and stabilisation process, not least though the work of its first presidents. The first, geneticist Victor McKusick, wrote the influential report on the prospects of the new genetics for the US National Academy of Science. The second, the molecular biologist Sydney Brenner, whose brainchild was HUGO, played a similar role for the Medical Research Council (MRC) and the Royal Society in the UK. Through HUGO, this small, but immensely influential, network of scientists sought to shape the research programme, so that mapping and sequencing were to become both the national and international objectives.

Initially, HUGO seemed to be stronger on agenda-making than delivery, not least regarding work on the ethical and social dimensions, and the European Science Foundation (1991) wrote a critical report. Arguably it is now more securely founded, and certainly has rather less opaque admission procedures.

While modern science makes global claims, the formation of these human genome research networks has primarily taken place in advanced capitalist societies. Despite a track record in molecular biology in the countries of the former Soviet Union, particularly Russia, the research system there is in such crisis that currently the lead players are the US, the UK, France and Japan (and in that order, according to the analysis carried out by Academia Europea). The US is massively the centre, with the others following some way behind.

Germany, despite its growing scientific strength, does not have a major role in this area. The continued presence of biologists who played an active part in the Nazi period as the directors of leading laboratories in the post-war period discredited German genetics research and fostered a revulsion against the new genetics. This revulsion was fed by new critical histories of genetics and biomedicine (Muller Hill, 1988; Weindling, 1989), effectively mobilised by the Green Party and taken by them into both *Länder,* and national debates, and internationally into the debates of the European Parliament. First, the Green Party effectively challenged the proposed name of the programme, Predictive Medicine. Then, after much bargaining, the Parliament gave its support to the genome programme providing that 7% of the budget was allocated to ethical, legal and social aspects (ELSA).

## Science Frictions?

Discussion of the HGP has been muted in the UK. Indeed, attempts to produce debates between scientists about a number of issues (e.g. John Durant's *Science Frictions* media series) have been conspicuous for their lack of liveliness, with scientists cosily agreeing with one another. In the UK, only the joint CIBA/Wellcome meeting in the spring of 1995 on the genetics of antisocial behaviour, with its perceived kinship to the 1992 US meeting on the genetics of violence which had been blocked as racist, has precipitated a public exchange, between scientists about the ethics and politics of such research (Hubbard, 1995). Unusually critical commentaries were run in most of the broadsheets, notably the *Independent,* where the conference was reviewed with hostility by ethologist Patrick Bateson, a review which, in turn, attracted a dismissive rejoinder by psychologist Michael Rutter, who had chaired the CIBA/Wellcome proceedings.

In contrast, very strong exchanges have taken place continuously within the US since the inception of the HGP. The *Science* editorial has served as a much-quoted milestone, in which the editor, Daniel Koshland (1989), claimed that the HGP would solve everything from schizophrenia and ageing to homelessness. The debate among US scientists was both public and acknowledged. In a subsequent issue of *Science,* Nobel prizewinner Salvador Luria (1989) robustly challenged the socio-technical agenda of the HGP. He argued that the project had been promoted by a 'self-serving coterie', and asked whether the Nazi programme to eradicate Jewish and otherwise 'inferior' genes by mass murder could be translated here into a gentler, kinder programme to 'perfect' human individuals by 'correcting' their genes in conformity to an ideal 'white Judeo-Christian economically successful' genotype.

While it is probably necessary to be a Nobel prizewinner to have such views published in a major scientific journal, even when there is a recognised controversy, feminist, liberal and left-wing critics of science in the US are ranged against the HGP, and have produced powerful critiques. These have gained sufficient cultural purchase that when the historian of eugenics, Daniel Kevles, and Leroy Hood, a leading figure within the HGP, jointly edited *The Code of Codes* (Kevles & Hood, 1992), it was felt appropriate to invite Evelyn Fox Keller to contribute as a distinguished feminist critic of science. However, neither the claims being made for the HGP nor the critics have remained constant. Few, following Luria's fundamentalist denunciation of Koshland's fantasy claims, have either advocated or attacked the HGP in quite these unequivocal terms.

However, while Keller is surely right that history does not repeat itself, it was surely equally an error to use the term 'Nazi conspiracy', as this serves to suggest that a minority of bad people (the Nazis) were involved, and that they rather successfully woodhinked the good (the majority). Yet the immense difficulty of confronting the Nazi period and eugenicism is that Nazi regimes with openly eugenicist programmes were popularly elected in both Germany and Austria, with only the communists, socialists and a handful of Christians - apart from the militant among their proposed victims - politically engaged against them.

## Eugenic Enthusiasms

While the Nazi episode stands as the historical embodiment of state eugenics in all its horror, it is important to recall a parallel enthusiasm for eugenics in most industrial countries, socialist as well as capitalist, which was supported by socially progressive scientists and social thinkers as well as by racists and reactionaries (Pickens, 1968; Weeks, 1981; Kevles, 1985). Nations were, however, rather different in the level at which they implemented their eugenicist enthusiasms. The US sterilised some 20 000 'feeble-minded' women; many of the Scandinavian countries had race laws disturbingly similar to those of Nazi Germany; while a number of UK social policy thinkers and biologists (for instance William Beveridge, Julian Huxley and J.B.S. Haldane) were very attracted to ideas of improving the race.

'Eutelegenis', the progressivists' version of eugenics, was seen by Haldane as being synonymous with socialism (Kevles, 1985). That the UK got little further than a policy of custodial care and sexual segregation for mentally impaired women and men may be a source of some relief; however, the point is that eugenicist ideas were actively discussed and endorsed. It was only the advent of the Nazi mass extermination of the mentally impaired and sick in the hospitals and the mass extermination of the death camps which silenced such dangerous enthusiasms for racial improvement. Such eugenicist histories and enthusiasms are, if not actually hidden, at least distinctly underplayed in national cultural self-accounting, leaving the Nazi episode to stand out as a singular horror story rather than as the monstrous epitome of a widespread current. Consequently, the current contrast with 'state eugenics' almost always set against the Nazi horror rather than this much more pervasive state eugenicism which lies uneasily, only half silenced, within the culture. As the repressed rather than the confronted, such histories threaten to return.

As recently as the 1970s, ironically at the height of the war on poverty which seemed to promise a fresh start in social policy, small numbers of 'feeble-minded' young black women were still being sterilised (Rose & Hanmer, 1976). Subsequently, Nixon's drive to screen for sickle cell anaemia, a genetic disease common among African Americans, led to extensive stigmatisation and employment discrimination. Rayna Rapp (1988), in her anthropological study of genetic counselling, observes that during the late 1980s, 99% of genetic counsellors were women and 95% were white. African American and sociologist Troy Duster shares Rapp's concerns, and is less confident that eugenicism is part of an unreturnable past. His study of the workings of genetic counselling in the lives of black and white Americans is not by chance entitled *Back Door to Eugenics* (Duster, 1990). For African Americans, it is not only a 'Nazi conspiracy' which gives cause for concern, US liberal democracy has its own negative record. As Duster observes: "Once again whether this new genetic knowledge is an advantage or a cross depends only partly on the how the genes are arranged. It depends as well where one is located in the social order". (Duster, 1990, p. 92).

Yet even for the apparently socially secure, the new genetics poses a historically new problem. As Dorothy Nelkin and Lawrence Tancredi document in their book *Dangerous Diagnostics* (Nelkin & Tancredi, 1994), the new genetics has proliferated tests but few therapies. Indeed, the diagnostic technology is integral to the development of the field, both in the sense of the technics of production of the knowledge and in a more directly commercial sense. While the HGP was launched to the sound of promises of gene therapy, and thus secured substantial investment from venture capital, the new diagnostics, even without therapies, offers to provide those promised returns. In so far as tests are offered to pregnant women, the only 'medical treatment' that can be proposed is abortion for fetuses deemed to be 'imperfect' (see Wheale and McNally in this book).

The response from ethically sensitive clinical geneticists, and from groups such as the King's Fund Consensus Forum (1987) on pre-natal screening, is to support the concept of choice, giving the pregnant woman the right to make the choice, supported by the best quality information and counselling. However, this assumes that a consensus supporting a woman's choice is ultimately available. In the US, this consensus is not present, not least because of fundamentalist Christianity's success in introducing the concept of personhood for the fetus - a success which affects abortion rights and more. While feminism was claiming agency for women, this powerful right-wing movement was claiming agency for what was described in another discourse as a bunch of cells. The cultural efficacy of claiming agency for the fetus cannot be ignored, even though its implications in law do not necessarily go along with the anti-abortion intentions of the protagonists. US lawyers have demonstrated their willingness to pursue cases of 'wrongful life' against doctors failing to provide tests for pregnant women, or against women failing to act on them.

## Voices in Opposition

As femininists have pointed out, the concept of 'choice', and indeed the entire discourse of 'reproductive rights', has come into difficulties (Petchesky, 1985). Two things have been important in this change. Firstly, reproductive science and technology were relatively low-status areas in the past, but they have undergone tremendous growth and are no longer meaningfully separated as two distinct areas; instead, they fuse as a powerful technoscience, which pervades the lives of women. Secondly, over the last 15 years, culture has taken a powerfully consumerist twist, as its most intense in the unregulated medical market economy of the US.

Following this line of analysis, geneticist Paul Billing, one of the critics associated with the US Council for Responsible Genetics, argues that the new danger stems precisely from the contemporary consumerist culture, so that choice becomes a highly problematic concept (Billings, 1994). In this culture (and I would add for the socially secure, which, given the Clinton failure to secure adequate nationwide health care, is likely still to exclude many million Americans), the new consumer eugenics replaces the old state eugenics. Thus different sections of US society, and particularly pregnant women in those different sections, are likely to find themselves challenged by very different kinds of eugenicism.

The Council, in part a rather more respectable offspring or the radical grouping Science for the People, includes a number of distinguished biologists who are both socially and scientifically concerned by recent developments in genetics. Over the years, leading figures, such as Jonathan Beckwith, Ruth Hubbard, Sheldon Krimsky and Richard Lewontin, have successfully punctuated the self-reported success story of the new genetics whether in its applications to green nature through biotechnology or to human nature. Among the more conspicuous recent examples of such interventions was Lewontin's challenge to the near absolutist truth claims being made for DNA 'fingerprinting'. The upshot from this intervention was that the claims made by experts advising law enforcement agencies were significantly modified (Lewontin, 1991). Usually, the intervention is made though a critical public understanding of science approach. Hubbards' contribution as both a feminist and biologist and her involvement with the women's health movement is a particularly good example. In a string of publications, she has set out to both demythologise the new genetics and to alert women to the imperialising claims of the new diagnostics (Hubbard, 1984, 1993, 1995). Despite the ambivalences which seem to exist between most new social movements and scientists, the challenge posed by the new genetics has led to a cautious regard for the scientists associated with the Council.

However, these robust, socially critical voices are not part of the progressional world of science, technology and society (STS) studies; they are outsiders, their legitimacy primarily lies within their molecular biology, theoretical biology or their biochemistry. These provide the cultural capital which amplifies their socio-technical criticism of the HGP. While academic STS studies in the US have not a strong normative agenda, individual STS scholars such as Nelkin, Tancredi and Duster have produced highly critical work which has nourished public debate. One consistent academic source of self-consciously normative criticism has been women's studies, with its peculiar location between the academy and the movement. Here, increasing numbers of feminists engaged in STS studies (including Anne Fausto Sterling, Evelyn Fox Keller, Donna Haraway, Sandra Harding and Rayna Rapp) have produced powerful critiques of aspects of the new genetics.

US critics of the HGP found little support in the institutionalised critical evaluation of science and technology policy. The US government Office of Technology Assessment (OTA), which many looked to with hope, turned itself into a facilitating agency when the HGP was proposed (see Robert Cook-Deegan's description of his role at the OTA:1994). Nonetheless, despite this handmaiden role to the HGP, the counter-revolution currently being waged by the Republicans threatens the continued existence of the OTA.

## UK Criticism

Voluntary associations in the UK equivalent to the Council for Responsible Genetics (CRG) have developed more weakly. Although the US is at the centre of the production system of modern science, UK molecular biological and genetic traditions are strong, and in principle there would seem to be a sufficiently self-confident cultural elite to ensure critical debate. However, this does not see to be the case. The Genetic Forum, while energetic within a small budget and involving a handful of activists, publishes a monthly publication - *The Splice of Life* - but does not command a distinguished line-up of biologists, not least geneticists. Like the majority of Green UK groups, but unlike the German Greens, the Forum focuses mainly on biotechnology: human genetics comes in a rather poor second.

Nor are there numbers of individual voices among the scientific community, raising strong socio-technical criticism against the HGP. Social criticism of science from the 1970s onwards has passed over to the muted tones of professional STS studies. To some extent, numbers of the current luminaries of STS were natural scientists, mobilised by the 1960s and 1970s radical science movement and then professionalised. The normativity of their earlier radicalism has been transformed into the intellectually radical project of the sociology of scientific knowledge, a project which, in a contradictory way, both intellectually nourishes and politically weakens more openly normative strategies. There are now few survivors of a past socially engaged tradition of radical scientists which extended, with a break for World War II and the Cold War, from the 1930s to the 1970s (Rose & Rose, 1976; Werskey, 1978). It is true that neurobiologist Steven Rose (1995) has recently criticised the US move into neurogenetics, and that ethologist Patrick Bateson was openly hostile to the CIBA/Wellcome meeting, but such public displays of unequivocal scientific dissent are increasingly rare in the UK.

Yet, the current vigour of the US debates and the UK mild disagreements are in marked contrast to the genetics debate of the 1930s, where UK geneticists were at the centre. The shift within the UK during the World War II was intense, nowhere more marked than in the anti-eugenicists politics of Lionel Penrose and his colleagues at University College. That he persuaded his colleagues to retitle his Chair in Eugenics to Human Genetics symbolised the marginalisation of the Galton Pearson tradition.

Today, Steve Jones, also of University College, is the most eloquent and widely read British geneticist. He is also unquestionably politically on the left. Nonetheless, his prizewinning *The Language of the Genes* (1993) shows little awareness of the dangers of a situation in which the new genetics can diagnose but not treat. He seems to believe that biomedical research is naturally in the best interest of the patients, and is clearly unaware of a substantial research literature which might challenge this. Nor does he critically reflect on the geneticisation of the culture which explains human diseases, disorders and behaviours in terms of genes. The 1995 MRC exhibition held at Euston Station, London ('Genes are Us') says it all. They, and by implication we, exist outside the social order.

The one unambiguous oppositional voice throughout the 1980s was that of the Feminist International Network against New Reproductive Technologies and Genetic Engineering (FINNRAGE). FINNRAGE, with particularly energetic figures in the UK such as Jalna Hanmer, has had considerable success in raising the issue of assisted reproduction and genetic engineering internationally, and not least in Europe in alliance with the German Green Party (Yoxen, 1983; Zipper & Sevenhuijsen, 1987).

Currently, it is a less audible voice. FINNRAGE's problems have been in its total opposition to both reproductive technology and genetic engineering, at the same time as many women, including number of feminists, were turning to the new technologies for help in overcoming problems of infertility or in their concern about inherited conditions. Thus, FINNRAGE was to become one of those organisations which recruit powerfully because of the radicalism of their critique, but which, because of the incompatibility of women's lived lives and the critique, also becomes a junction point, through which many feminist pass, rather than a destination. Numbers of feminists joined, but passed on their way to still critical, but rather more complex political positions, frequently entering feminists STS studies. Here, because of the successful institutionalisation of women's studies, they have been able to maintain a normative agenda which has been largely lost by mainstream STS (Stacey, 1992).

## The Peculiarity of UK Science Frictions

If the HGP is not central to national science frictions, what is? Unquestionably, the big UK debate about nature is the issue of animal rights and welfare, usually versus the experimental biologists, though currently the livestock exporters are demonised over and above them. Defending animals against cruelty is not new, but has bubbled through the national culture, emerging from time to time, not least since the birth of animal experimentation with physiology in the 1870s. Unquestionably this is now a strong cultural current, reflected, for example, in several pieces in the *New Statesman*, the advertised commitment of the Co-operative Bank not to invest in repressive regimes or, like the Body Shop, in animal experimentation for cosmetics. It increasingly automatically assumes that no sensitive, caring person can be anything other than a defender. For feminism, the history of opposition to vivisectionism has been more constant, though by no means commanding a consensus among either past or present feminists, but where in the nineteenth century violence against women was commonly linked to cruelty to animals, today's struggles are culturally and politically distinct.

Despite this popularity, the animal rights movement has some uncomfortable links with Nazism. The animal welfare legislation still current in Germany was initially introduced by the Nazis, and a concern with nature is an important stand of Nazi ideology. Even today, the November the Ninth Group (the Nazi Crystal Night) has been active in the UK within animal rights, although not without internal protest. Contemporary deep ecology's exclusion of human animals from the concept of nature and the attack on speciesism raise similar difficulties for those all too aware of the history of national socialism's nature politics.

If the epicentre of today's nature politics is animal rights, then this gives social scientists who are interested in a critical approach to STS particular problems. It is actually difficult for the UK debate to share the energy which comes from the US scene; instead the danger is that UK, and perhaps European, social science becomes acceptance science devoted to ironing out the ELSA problems of genetics as an innovative tehnoscience. Should we be more cautious about, and therefore deconstruct, the concepts of 'acceptability' and 'demand' which scatter both the ELSI and the ELSA literature, not least the programmes within which social science has to couch its requests.

## The Limits of Social Science or a Limited Social Science?

In the UK, there is no OTA with a clear (if on the HGP disregarded) brief, although parliamentarians in the House of Commons have the Parliamentary Office of Science and Technology (POST) and the European Union Parliament has Science and Technology Assessment (STOA). While both POST and STOA offer scientific support, how far this support is informational and how far it assists with critical technology assessment is unresolved. The belief that what parliamentarians need are the scientific facts, and that these will somehow speak for themselves, dies hard.

Within the UK, it is the MRC, like the NIH in the US, that is managing the ELSA programme for the HGP, and which also acts as the link for the European Framework programme. However, there are crucial differences in the

UK. Not only is the committee considering applications for ELSA chaired by a biologist, thus not reproducing the disciplinary independence of the US ELSI, but the person concerned is the manifestly partisan figure of the embryologist Lewis Wolpert, who has engaged in public debate with leading sociologists of science during 1994 at the British Association Meeting, in the columns of the *Times Higher Education Supplement*, and the Durham Meeting on the social status of science.

It is important to say something about Wolpert's views because of his key location within both ELSA and the Royal Society's Committee for the Public Understanding of Science (COPUS). He reads the strong constructionists, notably Harry Collins, not merely as a relativist but as fostering anti-science. That his reading misses most of the differences between sociologists, and, of course, ignores, as do mainstream sociologists, feminist work where a number of people (i.e. Birke, Cockburn, Harding, Haraway, Keller and Rose) cling to some version of objectivity in a way he should find quite endearingly conservative, is beside the point. What is peculiar to the UK situation is that someone with no expertise in ethics, law or the social sciences, who is on public record as hostile to the last, was felt to be appropriate to chair the UK committee to manage the ELSA programme.

Wolpert took over the chair of COPUS from the geneticist and erstwhile president of HUGO, Sir Walter Bodmer. Both hold the view that if the experts tell the public about the facts of science, then science will move back into public esteem, and public will be able to make better informed decisions about science. However, 'understanding' in this model equals 'knowledge of scientific facts'. Despite the Economic and Social Research Council (ESRC) programme on the public understanding of science, which showed that with increased scientific knowledge came increased willingness to evaluate and criticise, this ideological commitment to the equation between information and trust has remained unchanged on the part of these influential actors.

For very few social scientists is the concept of 'understanding' interchangeable with factual knowledge, in a non-positivist epistemology understanding is profoundly linked to meaning. Indeed, the ESRC qualitative studies of understanding science pointed to the ways in which different publics made sense of scientific knowledge alongside other equally important knowledges of everyday life (Irwin & Wynne, 1996). At a time when the wider culture increasingly recognises the limits of science and that science itself is socially shaped, this defence of science as being independent from society feels like a nostalgic throwback to a time when science was able to claim much greater authority.

In the current highly conservative and dirigistic UK climate, this account describes a particular move from within science to contain social criticism of science. Having begun with an attempt to abolish the Social Science Research Council in the early 1980s, the Conservative Party has settled down to a highly interventionist relationship with social science. This has been particularly marked where its conclusions are not congruent with government policies: the 1980s struggle to secure rights of publication for Department of Health supported research; Howard's more recent treatment of the Home Office Criminology Unit; to the censoring of Social Trends and the recent interference with Barnado's research on poverty in childhood.

However. in addition to the politics of the government, natural science in this country has also had a complicated relationship with social science (it is at least part of that Anglo Saxon problem in which science equals natural science, and we lack the concept of *Wissenschaft* as equalling all systematic knowledge). Thus, while some natural scientists defend the autonomy of the social sciences, there is still a widely held belief in the necessary subordination of social sciences under a positivistic programme. The MRC's long-standing commitment to quantitative research and its preference for preferably quantified social psychology over and above sociology is a continuing expression of this handmaiden view of the social sciences. This is not to suggest that the MRC-supported research in this area is socially uncritical. We do need detailed accounts of how diagnostic tests work out for different groups, for people at different points in their lives, such as having a baby, trying to get a job or take out insurance, but also for very different genetic conditions, not least whether immediate or late onset. The question is whether and how far such micro-social research is able to influence the existing actor network of the molecular biologists, the geneticists and industry. Such a network presently finds expression and support in such measures as the government Technology Foresight exercise. This technology-driven exercise asks the constructors of the new technosciences questions that would seem to require the skills of social science to answer, not least whether they anticipate social opposition to possible technological developments.

The UK response to the HGP is part of a deep-rooted cultural difficulty in coping with democratic debate about matters which involve high levels of technical expertise. Instead of a willingness to be open with the public, and accept that specific technological developments may be rejected, there is a desire to determine the outcomes. This means controlling who, and holding what values, is to be permitted to enter the actor networks. Such an institutionalised anxiety to control was demonstrated in the pioneering (for UK) consensus forum on biotechnology, held at Imperial College in 1994 and funded by the Biotechnology and Biological Sciences Research Council. Participants were, however, informed that they were not permitted to write a minority report. In contrast, in a similar technology assessment exercise in Germany which deliberately recruited a wider range of people and positions, members of the Green Party walked out. This was not seen as a failure, but as a fair expression within the political task of technology assessment (Van den Daele, 1994).

It is precisely the outsider groups, in the UK particularly the disability movement, which currently offer an energetic opposition to the new genetics. This needs to be brought into debates. The movement's challenge to the twin assumption that all would-be parents want a normal baby, and that biomedicine is able to define normality, disrupts the quiet and naturalised eugenicism of the dominant culture of the very late twentieth century. To say this is not to subscribe to everything proposed by the disability movement, which, at times, has come dangerously close to anti-abortion politics, nor is it necessary to ignore the popular support for the new genetics (from many families with children suffering genetic diseases) as offering the most likely means of finding new and effective therapies. Nonetheless, bringing this quiet and naturalised eugenicism into the foreground provides a crucial additional location from which the HGP requires assessment.

Though it is difficult, for the reasons I have tried to set out in a UK context, it is time to put the gains from STS together with the very diverse social concerns about the HGP. Sociologists and historians have spent two immensely rewarding decades delineating the actor networks which shape both scientific knowledge and technological artefacts. Although most of the work has had a non-normative agenda, the very idea of a socially shaped science and technology has opened the door to a self-consciously normative project of reshaping, to the possibility of a differently constructed science and technology. Expanding the networks, so that new actors enter through new institutions for technology assessment so that different and probably even more complicated conversations take place, are key to such a process.

## References

Billings, P. (1994) Contribution to an international seminar on Technology Assessment of Neurogenetics, January, Hamburg University.

Bodmer, W. & McKie, R. (1994) *The Book of Man,*. Little, Brown & Co., New York, NY, USA.

Callon, M. (1987) Society in the making: the study of technology as a tool for sociological analysis. In Bijker, W., Highes, T. & Pinch, T. (eds) *The Social Construction of Technological Systems*. MIT Press, Cambridge, MA, USA.

Cook-Deegan, R. (1994) *The Gene Wars,* 4th edn. Norton, New York.

Duster, T. (1990) *Back Door to Eugenics.* Routledge, New York, NY, USA.

European Science Foundation (1991) *Report on Genome Research.* European Science Foundation, Strasbourg.

Green, J. (1990) *Calming or Halming? A Critical Overview of Pschological Effects of Foetal Diagnosis in Pregnant Women,* Vol. 2, Galton Institute Occasional Papers.

Hubbard, R. (1984) Prenatal diagnosis and eugenic idealogy. *Women's Studies International Forum,* **8**, 567-576.

Hubbard, R. (1995) *Profitable Promises: Essays on Women, Science and Health.* Common Courage Monroe, ME, USA.

Hubbard, R. & Wald, E. (1993) *Exploding the Gene Myth.* Beacon, Boston, MA, USA.

Irwin, A. & Wynne, B. (eds) (1996) *Mis-understanding Science: Making Sense of Science and Technology in Everyday Life.* Cambridge University Press, Cambridge.

Jones, S. (1993) *The Language of the Genes.* Harper Collins, London.

Jordan, B. (1993) *Travelling Around the Human Genome.* Inserm, Paris.

Keller, E.F. (1992) Nature, nurture and the human genome project. In Kevles, D. & Hood, L. (eds) *The Code of Codes: Scientific and Social Issues in the Human Genome Project.* Harvard, Cambridge, MA, USA.

Kevles, D. (1985) *In the Name of Eugenics: Genetics and the Uses of Human Heredity.* Knop, New York, NY, USA.

Kevles, D. & Hood, L. (eds)(1992) *The Code of Codes: Scientific and Social Issues in the Human Genome Project.* Harvard U.P., Cambridge, MA, USA.

Kings Fund (1987) *Screening for Foetal and Genetic Abnormality. Consensus Statement.* Kings Fund Centre, London.

Koshland, D. (1989) Editorial. *Science,* **246**, 189.

Lewontin, R.C. (1991) *Biology as Ideology: The doctrine of DNA.* Harper, New York, NY. USA.

Luria, S. (1989) Letter. *Science,* **246**, 873.

Muller Hill, B. (1988) *Murderous Science: Elimination by Scientific Selection, Jews Gypsies and Others, Germany 1933-45.,* Clarendon Press, Oxford.

Nelkin, D. & Tancredi, L. (1994) *Dangerous Diagnostics,* Basic Books, New York.

Petchesky, R. (1985) *Abortion and Woman's Choice: The State, Sexuality and Reproductive Freedom.* Northeastern University Press, Boston, MA, USA.

Pickens, D.K. (1968) *Eugenics and the Progressives.* Vanderbilt University Press, Nashville, TN, USA.

Rapp, R. (1988) Chromosomes and communication: the discourse of genetic counsellors. *Medical Anthropology Quarterly,* **2**, 143-157.

Rose, S. (1995) The rise of neurogenetic determinism. *Nature,* **353**, 280-281.

Rose, H. & Hanmer, J. (1976) Women's liberation, reproduction and the technological fix. In Barker, D.L. & Allen,S. (eds) *Sexual Divisions and Society.* Tavistock, London.

Rose, H. & Rose, S. (eds) *(1976) The Radicalisation of Science.* Macmillan, London.

Shakespeare, T. (1995) Eugenics by the backdoor? The disability movement's concerns with the new genetics. Paper given at the Edinburgh International Science Festival, April.

Stacey, M. (ed.) (1992) *Changing Human Reproduction: Social Science Perspectives.* Sage, London.

Van den Daele, W. (1994) Technology Assessment as a Political Experiment. Wissenschafzentrum Berlin für Social Forschung (WZB), Berlin, Germany.

Weeks, J. (1981) *Sex, Politics and Society.* Tavistock, London.

Weindling, P, (1989) *Health, Race and German Politics between National Unfication and Nazism: 1870-1945.* Cambridge University Press, Cambridge.

Werskey, G. (1978) *The Visible College.* Penguin, Harmondsworth.

Yoxen, E. (1983) *The Gene Business: Who Should Control Biotechnology?* Pan Books, London.

Zipper, J. & Sevenhuijsen, S. (1987) Surrogacy: feminist notions of motherhood reconsidered. In Stanworth, M. (Ed.) *Reproductive Technologies: Gender, Motherhood, and Medicine.* Polity, Cambridge.

# 10  Signs of Life - Taking Genetic Literacy Seriously

JON TURNEY

ABSTRACT    *Genetic literacy is coming into use as a shorthand term for the educational goals of the Human Genome Programme. This chapter examines the motives of some of the main proponents of genetic literacy, and their views (implicit or explicit) about how it might be defined. It is suggested that prevailing models of genetic literacy share the flaw of the parent concept-scientific literacy-in its use as a shorthand for the requirements of a general public understanding of science. That is, they are top-down, prescriptive models, which assume that scientists and other experts get to define what people need to know. I then discuss whether the term can be modified for use in contexts where people who might need access to genetic information play a role in defining what they want to know, and how they can be helped to find out. This is related to future research in the field.*

## Introduction

The term 'genetic literacy' (or DNA) literacy is coming into use as a shorthand for the background knowledge any citizen ought to have access to when dealing with decisions relating to the new genetics (Childs & Hickman, 1983; Bodmer & McKie, 1994).    Just as some generalised idea of scientific and technological literacy is seen as a desirable goal in debates about the application of new genetic technologies.  However, the term is obviously problematic, just as the wider notion of scientific literacy is problematic.  This chapter examines the prospects for deriving something useful from the suggestion that we try to think about genetic literacy, and considers how the idea might be explored through research.

First, a few brief comments are made about the debate over scientific literacy, and then how this might relate specifically to genetics is examined. Finally, some elements of a research programme are proposed, designed to introduce a 'bottom up' element into the discussion and effect a partial escape from the prescriptive cast of most specifications of scientific literacies.

## From Scientific Literacy to Genetic Literacy

Scientific literacy had been discussed for around 20 years, although the related debate is, of course, much older than this. There is a whole range of arguments which have been advanced for promoting scientific literacy (Thomas & Durant, 1987). They are basically the same set as those used in favour of efforts to increase public understanding of science. But on a scale from public appreciation of science (a term favoured by some), though public understanding of science to scientific literacy, the last is the most challenging term. It appears to demand some kind of detailed specification, by analogy with general literacy, which is concerned with a particular capability.

These specifications have almost always been top-down formulations, and are framed prescriptively-even when they are claimed not to be. They are implicitly or explicitly about what people need to know, or should know, about science and technology.

Today, there seems to be agreement that what individuals should know is not restricted to factual knowledge, although some books exist which embody a fact-based notion of scientific literacy (Brennan, 1992; Trefil, 1992). Most commentators now offer definitions of scientific literacy which include a range of elements designed to reflect scientific process (Durant, 1994). Again , the details may differ. A.B. Arons, for example, has a 12-point specification which would add up to a fairly substantial introductory course in the history and philosophy of science (Arons, 1983). However, the important point is that while still prescriptive, these accounts of scientific literacy extend to the nature of science, as well as taking in aspects of what they usually still call, in the language of the 1960s, the impact of science on society.

Genetics has had some prominence in earlier debates about scientific literacy, particularly with respect to scientific facts and social impact. This has largely been through the efforts of people associated with the Biological Sciences Curriculum Study (BSCS) in the US, one of the post-Sputnik curriculum reform organisations which is still very active.

For example, when *Daedalus* devoted an issue to scientific literacy in 1983, genetics was only one of two specific subjects to have an essay to itself (the other was computers). Barton Childs and Faith Hickman outlined a scheme for revitalising biology teaching in schools, using human genetics to promote student interest. It is worth noting that, while they obviously felt that genetics was important, they saw its importance as a vehicle for promoting general scientific literacy, rather than emphasising the need to understand genetics in its own right (Childs & Hickman, 1993).

Hickman has earlier been part of a BSCS team which fielded a 64-item questionnaire aimed at probing high school and college students' knowledge of, and attitudes towards, genetics (Hickman *et al.*, 1978). Since the advent of the Human Genome Programme, the BSCS has been in the forefront of the education effort focused on the 'new genetics', developing a text and software package designed to teach students how to use a DNA database, for instance (BSCS, 1994).

This kind of approach is no doubt appropriate for schools, but if applied to the wider public it is subject to the same kinds of criticism which have been levelled at the simpler notions of scientific literacy. Ever since the Royal Society's report on public understanding of science appeared in 1985, it has been apparent that each of the three terms in the key phrase, 'public', 'understanding' and 'science' needs unpacking in some detail when any particular problem is addressed. Most academic writers in this area now emphasise the importance of considering 'knowledges in context', rather than some abstract ideal of public understanding of science, in which the task implicity set for the laity is to learn to reproduce scientific accounts of situations or phenomena at whatever level they are capable of (Wynne, 1991). In practice, people try to acquire 'science for specific social purposes' (Layton *et al.*, 1992). Also, as Joan Solomon puts it, "Scientific knowledge needs to be partnered with complementary social understandings, even at the expense of conceptual purity, if it is to become usable as citizen knowledge" (Solomon, 1992).

In this light, ideas about scientific literacy often seen inseparable from a simple 'deficit' model of public understanding of science, which is top-down and prescriptive, and assumes that the understanding that lay publics should have is, in its essentials, identical to that of scientists. The more recent discussion of genetic literacy is also in danger of passing the insights of a more contextual approach to understanding.

This is partly because, at one level, it is obviously true that more people will find themselves in situations where they may want access to some kind of genetic knowledge. As the HGP gathers momentum, more and more non-geneticists are going to have to make sense of the new information being generated. Genetic screening will be more widely applied, for example, and will move out of conventional counselling contexts. It will also affect personal decisions outside the reproductive realm which has defined most of our experience of such tests so far. In additions, it will more often be applied to conditions whose aetiology is much more complex than the simple Mendelian cases which have attracted the most attention in this area to date. A test for propensity to heart disease in adults, for example, along the lines of the currently available proprietary home cholesterol test, would raise very different problems of understanding and decision than a pre-natal test for cystic fibrosis (Linnan *et al.*, 1990).

In relation to genetic engineering, what people understand about the technologies of genetic manipulation, and what they believe will be possible-in terms of gene therapy, in particular-will affect their attitudes to screening, as well as to regulation of new genetic research and its implications.

Those close to the field know all this, of course, and it is implicit in many of the calls for developing genetic literacy which we are now hearing. In the discussion of genetics, and specifically human genetics, the view that improvements in public understanding are desirable is very widespread. At its grandest, it gives rise to statements like Nancy Wexler's that "rather than slow the science, we need to accelerate the creation of a social system that will be more hospitable to new information about our genes, our heritage and our future" (quoted in Cooper, 1994).

This view seems to have three main motives. One is that, as the HGP bears fruit, more people will need to make sense of information about the results of screening tests, for example. As the Nuffield Council on Bioethics report put it: "If an individual is to be well enough informed to be able to give consent to genetic screening, he or she needs to have some general understanding of genetics. This means that the public as a whole needs to have a greater knowledge and awareness of the genetic processes that can affect us all" (Nuffield Council on Bioethics, 1993).

Aside from individuals' ability to give informed consent (or, presumably, decline to do so), there is a wider need for understanding to inform policy-making in this area. Again, this is highlighted in the Nuffield report: "A broad public understanding of the scientific basis of medical genetics is essential if informed public policy decisions are to be taken about the introduction of genetic screening programmes".

Finally, there is an interest on the researchers' part in a different facet of policy-making, the regulation and oversight of work in the laboratory and its application-from environmental release of genetically modified organisms to protocols for trials of human gene therapy. At this level, there is concern about improving public understanding to ensure that the research is permitted at all. This concern is quite prominent in some areas of the life sciences. As Sir Ralph Riley put it, succinctly, "There is often insufficient understanding of genetics for rational judgments to be made of its effects" (Riley, 1993), although the record suggests that when there are particular threats to research, the scientific community can be very effective at mobilising to fight them off, as shown by the parliamentary debate about embryo research, for example (Mulkay, 1994).

Motives aside, these official or scientific views typically envisage a more elaborate specification of genetic literacy as deriving form a more systematic consideration by those who already have appropriate scientific knowledge. In the US, for example, the 1993 Institute of Medicine Report on Assessing Genetic Risks devotes a chapter to public education in genetics. This group call for education programmes "intended to develop a genetically literate public that understands basic biological research, understands elements of the personal and health implications of genetics, and participates effectively in public policy issues involving genetic information" (Institute of Medicine, 1993).

They went on: *"Genetics professionals and qualified educators* must assume responsibility for identifying the essential components of genetic literacy. What do *we* want people to know, value, and do about genetic information" (emphasis added).

Even accepting this, arriving at a consensus about what parts of this very complex science people should know about might not be easy. As soon as you start trying to define in detail what elements of genetic literacy defined in these terms might be, the exercise quickly becomes very elaborate, as I have argued elsewhere (Turney, 1995).

However, this is only the start of the difficulty. More important is that the argument that it is only worth considering knowledge in context in any serious discussion of public understanding of science applies to genetics as much as to any other area of science. As Rayna Rapp has repeatedly emphasised in her studies of genetic counselling from a cultural anthropological point of view, "While the language of science claims to be universal, it must, in fact, confront the local idioms with which diverse groups and individuals respond to its powerful messages" (Rapp, 1988). In a later paper drawing on the same material, she elaborates on how the unequal encounter between prior beliefs and scientifically sanctioned ideas about genetics is managed, emphasising the 'discursive work' that the construction of a scientific view of heredity entails: "Not only must popular meanings of hereditary transmission be suppressed in favour of scientific ones; scientific meanings must also be made sufficiently accessible so that patients (in this case pregnant women and their supporters) can act upon them" (Rapp, 1992). At their simplest, such ideas imply that we pay close attention to such questions as who might need to know what, for what purpose and who is defining their need and prescribing how it might be met?

Others with a more sophisticated view of understanding are making the same point. Some argue on the basis of work in the clinic, as in Richards' developing study of lay beliefs in relation to familial breast cancer (Richards, 1993). Other views are based on more general studies of public knowledge of and attitudes towards the new human genetics. Durant and colleagues, for example, point out that the public understanding of genetics can be considered as a conceptual space populated with a great variety of actors and actor groups, who include researchers, clinicians, counsellors, patients and their families, lawyers, journalists, special interest groups, policy-makers and politicians (Durant *et al.*, 1995).

In addition there are a small number of studies which show directly that scientific or medical professionals' views of the information most likely to be of use to lay people in particular genetic contexts are likely to be some way off the mark. They include Myers and colleagues comparing consumers' views about the best way to run an educational programme for cystic fibrosis carrier screening with professional prescriptions for the same programme (Myers *et al.*, 1994); Layton's work with parents of newborn Down's syndrome children; and Rose and Lambert's study of the information sources used by individuals and families managing hypercholesterolaemia (Laton *et al.*, 1992; Lambert and Rose, 1996). In the latter two cases, the significance of the genetic details of the conditions under discussion often disappeared for people trying to solve immediate, practical problems for which genetic knowledge had little or no relevance-a finding which is in line with other recent qualitative studies on understanding science.

## Implications for Future Research on Genetic Literacy

What implications might these considerations have for future research on genetic literacy? There is a good deal of work either already accessible in the literature or under way which focuses on what people already know about genetics, which I have reviewed elsewhere. What remains an open question is not so much what do people know about genetics, but what do they want to know?

If we want to discover if the idea of genetic literacy has any merit in this context, three further questions arise. Is there any professional consensus about the detailed requirements for genetic literacy? How well do existing efforts to impart genetic knowledge in books or other media productions serve lay audiences? How might definitions of genetic literacy by different actors be related?

One might begin by reviewing the various literatures on the public understanding of genetics, and educational, popular and professional works on human and medical genetics and genetic manipulation to define the range of items which might be part of genetic literacy. They include knowledge of facts and understanding of concepts in genetics (both classical and molecular genetics), acquaintance with the scientific process in research in this area, knowledge of technical possibilities likely to emerge from current or foreseeable research, as well as awareness of issues in a range of debates on the significance of genetic information and its social, legal or ethical importance. More general understanding of, for example, risk, chance and probability, would also figure in this review, as would knowledge of the history of genetics and its uses.

The point of this would be to define as wide a range of headings as possible for use in elucidating the view of various interested parties on the uses of genetic information. They would include professionals of various kinds, who would be asked not what *they* know, but what they believe the public might need to know to help them reach decisions about genetics and genetic engineering. How, for example, do academic geneticists, clinicians, genetic counsellors, psychologists, health educators and patients' organisations conceive knowledge and understanding which might be needed for different purposes? Is there any core of items which begins to look like a consensual definition of genetic literacy?

In addition, it would also be crucial to explore notions of genetic literacy among lay groups of various kinds. As the technology of testing is developing rather rapidly, it will be important to incorporate a prospective element in any such discussions, perhaps by posing plausible genetic scenarios to focus groups. The aim would be to establish what members of each group feel they need to know to be comfortable with their view of an issue, or with their ability to enter discussion about the new genetics. The discussion would also consider how they would prefer to acquire such information, what sources they would have confidence in, and whether they would consider devoting any effort to becoming better informed about these subjects in advance.

There are two reservations about this approach. Focus groups are recognised as an effective qualitative research method, but are generally used to record discussion of issues the members are already broadly familiar with (Morgan, 1988). A prospective discussion may be more subject to group effects which compromise the analysis. In addition, there is often a gap between people's perception of their hypothetical wants and their actual wants if they encounter the situation discussed.

For these reasons, the focus group work would probably need to be integrated with individual interviews of two kinds. One group of interviews would cover the same ground as the focus groups as a check on possible group effects. The second will involve people who have actually faced at least one of the situations discussed, for comparison with the results from the group who were invited to consider the same situation as only a possibility.

One can only speculate at this stage what might emerge from such a study. But it seems likely that it would reveal increasing transformations of 'scientific' accounts of genetic information as discussion moves from 'upstream' to 'downstream' contexts, to adopt the terminology Hilgartner has proposed for considering general arguments about science communication and popularisation (Hilgartner, 1990). This terminology has the advantage that it suspends judgement about correctness or accuracy, and emphasises that one should accept that knowledge is always transformed when it is communicated, and that the key judgment is what transformation is appropriate for each context-popular or professional.

The outcome, of course, might be that the notion of genetic literacy proves unworkable-that the knowledge of people indicate they wish to have, and the form they want it in, differs so much from context to context, and is at such variance with professionals' prescriptions, that there are too few common features to work with. Nevertheless, it seems worthwhile taking the exploration of genetic literacy further in this way, even while recognising that the idea is as problematic as indicated. If the concept does come apart in the course of further research, that itself will be an important conclusion to take back to the technical experts, who may otherwise continue to advocate education programmes based on an unexamined notion of genetic literacy.

## Acknowledgements

The work described in this chapter is supported by grants from the Wellcome Trust.

## References

Arons, A. (1983) Achieving wider scientific literacy. *Daedalus*, **112**, 91-122.
Bodmer, W. & McKie, R. (1994) *The Book of Man: The Quest to Discover our Genetic Heritage*. Little, Brown and Co., London.
Brennan, R. (1992) *Dictionary of Scientific Literacy*. John Wiley, Chichester.
BSCS (1994) *The Human Genome Project: Information Management, Access and Regualtion*, field test version. BSCS, Boulder, CO, USA.
Childs, B. & Hickman, F. (1983) Human genetics: one approach to scientific literacy. *Daedalus*, **112**, 189-209.

Cooper, N. (ed.) 1994) *The Human Genome Project: Deciphering the Blueprint of Heredity.* W.H. Freeman, Los Angeles, CA, USA.

Durant, J. (1994) What is scientific literacy? In Durant, J. & Gregory, J. (eds) *Science and Culture in Europe.* Science Museum, London, 129-138.

Durant, J., Hansen, A. & Bauer, M. (1995) Public understanding of the new genetics. In Marteau, T. & Richards, M. (eds) *The Troubled Helix.* Cambridge University Press, Cambridge.

Hickman, F., Kennedy, A. & MacInerny, J. (1978) Human genetics education: result of BSCS Needs Assessment Surveys. *The American Biology Teacher,* **38,** 285-308.

Hilgartner, S. (1990) The dominant view of popularisation: conceptual problems. Political uses. *Social Studies of Science,* **20,** 519-539.

Institute of Medicine (1993) *Assessing Genetic Risks. National Academy of Sciences,* Washington, DC, USA.

Lambert, H & Rose, H. (1996) Disembodied knowledge? Making sense of medical science. In Irwin, A. & Wynne, B. (eds) *Misunderstanding Science.* Cambridge University Press, Cambridge.

Layton, D., Kenkins, E., MacGill and Davey, A. (1992) *Inarticulate Science? Perspectives on the Public Understanding of Science and Some implications for Science Education.* Studies in Education Ltd, Driffield.

Linnan, L., Gans, K., Hixson, M., Mendes, E., Longpre, H. & Carleton, R. (1990) Training health professionals and lay volunteers to deliver cholesterol screening and education programs. *Public Health Reports,* **105,** 589-598.

Morgan, D. (1988) *Focus Groups as Qualitative Research.* Sage, Newbury Park, CA, USA.

Mulkay, M. (1994) Embryos in the news. *Public Understanding of Science,* **3,** 33-53.

Myers, M., Bernhardt, B., Tambor, E. & Holtzman, N. (1994) Involving consumers in the development of an educational program for cystic fibrosis carrier screening. *American Journal of Human Genetics,* **54,** 719-726.

Nuffield Council on Bioethics (1993) *Genetic Screening-Ethical Issues.* Nuffield Foundation, London.

Rapp, R. (1988) Chromosomes and communication: the discourse of genetic counselling. *Medical Anthropology Quarterly,* **2,** 143-157.

Rapp, R. (1992) *Heredity, or: Revising the Facts of Life.* Paper delivered to the American Anthropological Association.

Richards, M. (1993) The new genetics: some issues for social scientists. *Sociology of Health and Illness,* **15,** 567-586.

Riley, R. (1993) Introduction. In Dixon, B. (ed.) *Genetics and the Understanding of Life, Proceedings of the XVIIIth International Congress of Genetics.* National Centre for Biotechnology Education, Reading.

Solomon, J. (1992) *Getting to know about Energy-in School and Society.* Falmer Press, Brighton.

Thomas, G. & Durant, J. (1987) Why should we promote the public understanding of science? *Scientific Literacy Papers,* Oxford University Department for External Studies, 1-15.

Trefil, J. (1992) *1001 Things Everyone Should Know about Science.* Cassell, London.

Turney, J. (1995) The Public Understanding of Genetics-Where Next? *European Journal of Genetics in Society,* **1**, 5-20.

Wynne, B. (1991) Knowledges in context. *Science, Technology and Human Values,* **16**, 111-121.